Kay Deward twenty-five and has worked within the field of property writing for over three years, having worked at *Homes Overseas* magazine before freelancing for them as well as *What House?* magazine, *Your New Home* and the *Independent*. She lives in Didsbury, Manchester.

NO GOING BACK

Buying Abroad

KATY POWNALL

timewarner
paperbacks

A *Time Warner* Paperback

First published in Great Britain in 2004
as a paperback original by Time Warner Paperbacks

Copyright © Channel 4 2004

All information in this book has been checked by the author and
publisher, but the reader is advised to make his or her own personal
investigations before embarking on any venture.

The moral right of the author has been asserted.

A CIP catalogue record for this book
is available from the British Library.

ISBN 0 7515 3625 3

Typeset in Sabon by M Rules
Printed and bound in Great Britain by Clays Ltd, St Ives plc

Time Warner Paperbacks
An imprint of
Time Warner Book Group UK
Brettenham House
Lancaster Place
London WC2E 7EN

www.twbg.co.uk

For James and my mum and dad
With thanks for your support and encouragement

If you are about to follow your dreams by opening a new business abroad or in the UK and would be interested in appearing in a future episode of *No Going Back*, then please contact the production company Ricochet on mail@ricochet.co.uk.

CONTENTS

CHAPTER 1

From Norfolk to Catalonia

Martin Kirby, Maggie Whitman, and their five-year-old daughter Ella were a solid part of the fabric of their village in Norfolk. They enjoyed frequent visits from friends and relations and a good income earned through careers they found rewarding. In fact, Martin and Maggie had everything that many people in middle England might regard as desirable but they decided it wasn't what they wanted. For this reason they left everything, and traded it for life on a crumbling Catalonian farm.

Things in Norfolk had been far from perfect. Martin, deputy editor of the *Eastern Daily Press*, would regularly find himself still in the office at one a.m., not returning home until two a.m. 'I loved my work but I was finding it increasingly difficult,' he explained. 'I was essentially working nights, so the time I had with Ella and Maggie was poor and I really feel like I missed out on a huge chunk of Ella's early years. I would get to bed by two a.m., sometimes three a.m., but then I would be up again at seven a.m. with Maggie to snatch a few precious hours with my family. My health was beginning to deteriorate, sleep deprivation meant my body was playing up, it was definitely trying to tell me something.'

A daydream began to take shape in Martin's mind – what if he didn't have to be driven by deadlines? Of all the things the family enjoyed in their seemingly idyllic existence, time wasn't one of them. Maggie had also been wondering how they could change the balance of their lives and when she fell pregnant for a second time these thoughts became more pressing. They both wanted to put more time and energy into themselves and their children, to have the freedom to make family life the priority. This was dovetailed with wanting their children to have outdoors space and freedom to grow up in, a good diet of home-grown fruit and vegetables and, most importantly, the undivided attention of both of their loving parents. Together Martin and Maggie decided that all these needs could be met by running a smallholding. 'We are both very hard-working people, and the driving force behind the idea of the change wasn't wanting to do less. In fact, we knew a smallholding would be hard physical labour – Maggie is a farmer's daughter and I spent much of my childhood working on farms, so we had a fair idea of what it would entail. We also wanted to be stimulated in new ways and the challenge was very alluring.'

So Martin and Maggie began hunting for semi-derelict smallholdings around Norfolk that they could restore. But it became clear that instead of reducing their mortgage they would have to extend it to be able to afford anything appropriate, and they would have to forsake the dream of Martin giving up work to write, and for them to run a business together. Of course, with the UK property market being what is was (and still is), and with Norfolk being a very desirable place to own property, they simply couldn't find anything. With precious little alternative, and an undeniable wave of excitement, their thoughts turned to foreign climes.

'Maggie's sister and her family were away in France and northern Spain working on farms. To stop the post from building up she had redirected her mail to us and so we were regularly receiving copies of the *Willing Workers on Organic Farms* newsletter. It was while idly flicking through this one day that something caught my eye – a beautiful organic farm near Toulouse in France, seven acres of land with a stream and an established weekly market stall in the nearby town . . . all for £48,000!'

Martin decided that he had to go and see it. Maggie readily agreed but, being quite heavily pregnant and with Ella in tow, it was decided that Martin should go out alone. He was due to go to Mozambique for his newspaper that week and so booked a visit to the farm for the weekend after.

'It was a masterclass in how not to research buying a property abroad,' Martin admits of his first viewing. 'I hadn't had the common sense to ask for a detailed description of the property, or even a picture. I had fallen in love with the notion of buying a farm abroad and had been temporarily blinded to the practicalities. The second that I arrived and actually looked at it, this realisation came crashing down and I could see it was wholly impractical for us. It

was an extremely remote mountainside farm, completely isolated and in need of a lot of work.'

Fortunately the kind couple selling the farm read Martin's
disappointed face in a flash and put him in contact with a
local estate agent who could show him some alternative
properties in the area. Desperate not to have wasted his time
and money and determined to have something positive to tell
Maggie when he got back, Martin raced around the
Garonne. It was the last property he saw that made his heart
leap: a derelict farm next to a quaint village on a scenic hilltop. The house occupied a stunning position overlooking
the church steeple and the village beyond. It also came with
a beautiful one-acre meadow, a solitary apple tree and a lot
of potential. With a price tag of just £27,000, there would be
plenty of spare cash to transform the farm. Excitedly, Martin
took a film full of pictures and bundled himself back on a
plane to rejoin Maggie and Ella.

'You've got to see it,' enthused Martin upon his return.
While Maggie agreed wholeheartedly she was, as she pointed
out to him, three weeks from having a baby. She simply
could not visit at that moment. As a stopgap the family made
do with a montage of the pictures of the house taken by
Martin pinned to the notice board in their kitchen. 'Even this
token effort made things seem a little more real,' said
Martin. 'Our aspirations were coming into focus, the house
we were potentially going to buy was there for friends and
family to see.'

In July 2000, just a month after the birth of baby Joe Joe,
Maggie valiantly fought her way onto a crowded plane on a
Norfolk runway, Martin at her side, Ella round her leg and
babe in arms . . . she was determined to see the house. While

most women would have been recuperating and adapting to life with another child, Maggie had become even more determined that she, Martin and Ella should change theirs as soon as humanly possible.

To make the somewhat awkwardly timed trip a little more pleasant, the family had arranged to fly to Girona in northern Spain to spend a couple of days with Maggie's sister, her partner Terry and their children Rosa and Leila who were staying with their good friends Mac and Conxita on a farm nearby. From there, they could easily drive to south-west France and view the property that Martin had seen, as well as look at a few more that were located in the vicinity.

After a horribly delayed flight, throughout which Ella and baby Joe Joe had behaved impeccably, they emerged onto the runway at Girona knowing that a long drive was ahead. At 11.25 that night their hire car pulled into the square of the small village and Martin called from a phone box to let Mac know that they had made it. In no time his old but much loved Land Rover had arrived, they all piled in and began the final, and by far the roughest, leg of their journey, up the muddy, mile-long track to Mac and Conxita's house. After greetings all round and a final feed for Joe Joe they collapsed, exhausted, into their allocated beds for the night.

The following morning when the shutters were opened, Martin and Maggie were quite simply blown away by the beauty of the place they had driven to in the dark. It was stunning; mountain after mountain loomed as far as the eye could see, dotted with ramshackle villages and vineyards. Over breakfast Mac and Conxita announced that they had found a few properties within their local area for Martin and Maggie to view. They politely agreed – thinking that, if nothing else, it would be handy to compare prices. It seemed a bit strange, though . . . they had their hearts set on France after all.

Even when I ask him now how the family ended up buying a house in Spain, Martin seems a little unsure: '. . . an extraordinarily freaky sequence of events . . .' is the closest he comes to putting his finger on it.

One of the properties they viewed that morning was an old run-down farmhouse with ten acres of land and a very recently erected 'For Sale' sign. The sandy-coloured walls of the main farmhouse came into view as the car bumped along the track. Each end of the building was finished with a symmetrical three-storey tower, and in the centre, above the two balconies, was a mottled sundial. The house was badly in need of work, the window frames were rotting and the walls were flaking, but it was habitable – the elderly owners Nuria and Enric were living testament to this. The walls and roof were solid, and the water and waste systems were in working order. The land itself was a tumultuous riot of overgrown terraces, olive and almond trees and a healthy crop of vines. The farm was called L'Hort de la Mare, which means Mother's Garden, and it tugged on Maggie and Martin's heartstrings, but at £95,000 (€141,933) – £35,000 (€52,292) over the family's budget – it seemed too expensive to contemplate.

Maggie and Martin continued their journey to France and looked at the properties they had arranged to see there, but although they were charming and the area was wonderful, it slowly dawned on them that to continue their search was futile; quite by accident they had fallen head over heels in love with Mother's Garden. Even the French property that they had dreamed about was nothing in comparison. With this decisive, and unpredicted, factor acknowledged, there was a lot for the couple to discuss and investigate. The checklist needed to be satisfied. As far as schools went, the local village contained a good one, and the headmaster, who spoke good English, lived next door to Mother's Garden. There was a twenty-four-hour medical centre three kilometres from the village which would provide for healthcare and almost everything could be bought at the small shops in the village. The house was in a seemingly remote, isolated valley yet the local village and town provided everything that Maggie and Martin could dream of needing. Barcelona was an hour and a half away for when the big city beckoned and, of course, their friends, and now potential neighbours, Mac and Conxita would be on hand to ease them into the Spanish life and language.

'It was perfect,' smiles Martin. 'It was almost as though fate was playing its part; we both had a very strong gut feeling that this was right. The only thing we had to worry about now was money.'

Mother's Garden was signed for and a £2,000 deposit was laid down. The family had until the end of August to complete, which did not present a problem as it was assumed that there would be no difficulty selling the Norfolk property. It was a pretty cottage in a sought-after village and with the UK property market going from strength to strength, it seemed they couldn't fail. Immediately after their return to England, the house was put on the market at £195,000.

The weeks ticked by . . . and nothing. To Martin's amazement and horror it seemed that no one was interested in their home. It became apparent that they were not going to have sufficient funds to complete the sale on Mother's Garden at the end of August. Mac and Conxita kindly offered to have a word with Enric and Nuria to explain the situation – this was done and an extension of an additional four weeks was readily offered to Maggie and Martin. They now had until the end of September to secure the funds. Beginning to feel the strain a little, the couple arranged for another estate agent to put their cottage on the books, but still . . . nothing.

Towards the end of September the panic began to set in. It became horribly apparent to both Martin and Maggie that for reasons beyond their control their own property – and sole source of capital – was not going to sell in time. By this stage additional pressure had been applied as Mother's Garden had another interested buyer, who was offering more money. Enric and Nuria had made it clear that if the family were not in Spain with the money to complete the sale for the last week of September, they would lose the house *and* their deposit.

Unwilling to admit defeat Martin and Maggie set out on a campaign to somehow accrue the money. Their £190,000 Norfolk property had just £70,000 of the mortgage outstanding and so was remortgaged so that the couple could use the equity. However, they were still left with a £35,000 shortfall – they needed lenders.

Within less than five days, amazingly, they had done it. Family had rallied round and it finally looked as though they would be able to buy their dream property. And so, with their respective mothers in tow, Martin and Maggie flew over to Spain to sign for their house. At this point it was still touch-and-go as to whether the money would have transferred without hitch to their new Spanish account, but strangely both were buoyed by a feeling that it would happen. And it did. By the end of the week Martin and Maggie were the proud owners of a run-down Spanish farm, a cottage in Norfolk and around £180,000 of debt.

'This realisation seriously undermined the euphoria we felt about actually getting the house,' admits Martin, 'but before long a contract race was under way for our Norfolk property and we exchanged. It was an extraordinary period of time for the whole family. We all suddenly realised the profound changes we had planned were real . . . that we were going. Even with all the setbacks, and nearly losing the property, a belief that it was the right thing to do kept us going. We just kept pushing at doors and they opened for us. I handed in my notice after twenty-two years at the *Eastern Daily Press* and on 15 January we set off.'

With legal fees and other costs covered, the family had just £10,000 with which to start their new life. It was decided that in order to save money they would make the move to Spain themselves – with a little help from their friends of course. The morning of the move a seven-tonne truck, a transit van, and a Range Rover equipped with roof rack and trailer, all loaded to capacity, set off on the two-day drive to Catalonia. Just a week later Martin, Maggie, Ella and Joe Joe were living in Mother's Garden.

The initial few months were far from easy. Naturally, their immediate priority was to make sure that Ella and Joe Joe were secure and settled. The children needed to get into the rhythm of life on a Spanish farm; to get their own measure of the community and Ella needed to be introduced to the school and the Catalan language. Fortunately young children are the most adaptable of creatures and both kids were delighted with their new lifestyle and surroundings. During any time not spent with the children Martin and Maggie's priority was the house, which, though habitable, needed work and in mid-January it was a trial to keep it warm. There were a lot of draughts to stop and a lot of wood to be cut. Maggie set about planting a vegetable patch which, once grown, might shave a little off their food bill as well as improving their diet. The next big job was the vines, of which there were some 800 to tend. After seeking some advice from the extremely friendly and helpful locals, and with the invaluable help of Mac and Conxita, they were able to prune and weed the vines. As they didn't believe in spraying and wanted to run the whole farm organically, this meant that each vine had to be individually nurtured by hand.

'It was back-breaking work,' recalls Martin, 'but good for the soul! Both Maggie and I were reminded daily by our bodies that we weren't as young as we used to be. I'd wake up stiff as an ironing board most days.'

As if the physical labour wasn't challenging enough there was also their own adjustment to be factored into the equation. With the children and farm labour taking up almost all of their time there was little opportunity for Martin and Maggie themselves to assimilate their new cultural, climatic and financial situation.

'It was extremely difficult,' says Martin. 'Although Maggie and I both have farming in our blood, growing any crop out here is different to back in the UK. Neither of us have had experience of this climate, or of crops such as vines and olive trees, which need quite specialised care. There was also a huge psychological adaptation to make, which Maggie grasped far sooner than I did. Coming from my nine-to-five existence, I was used to having a set structure to my day where I knew what I would be doing and where I should be. For those first few months on the farm, each day was like a blank canvas to be filled. The amount of work that needed to be done was so daunting that I just couldn't prioritise – I kept asking Maggie what I should do. In the end she gave me exactly what I needed and told me in no uncertain terms that I had to start using my own initiative.'

Martin admits that he also had problems relaxing about the fact that they had no regular income.

'Our economies of scale had drastically altered overnight. It was a very strange feeling knowing there was no regular source of money. Equally, though, there was no urgent need for worry as our outgoings were absolutely minimal too. We had bought the house outright so there was no mortgage to worry about. The cost of living is cheaper and from the beginning we were able to provide many of the basics from our own land. There are minimal transport costs as we don't really need to go anywhere, no refuse charges as we take our own rubbish to the tip, and no water rates as our water comes from our own spring.

'There was plenty of work to be done on the house but we had some spare money that we could use for that and, as we gradually earned from our crops, we got things done a little at a time. I also became the king of scavenging – seeking out everything from sinks and cupboards to gas cookers.'

'As well as all this change and tumult there was the added

pressure of my mother being gravely ill. Shortly before we moved out to Catalonia she suffered a stroke and lost her ability to communicate to a great extent. This added a huge amount of guilt to the move. Could I bear to leave my mother in this state in England? She had other family around her but it was still a terrible decision to have to make. In the end I knew that we had to move – my mother had been so enthusiastic about our plans and she loved Spain. Her illness lasted a further eighteen months before she died, during which time I made ten return trips to England to visit her, which was hard for both Maggie and myself. My stepfather also passed away around this time.'

It was hard graft and an emotional roller coaster, but in spite of all the problems things gradually began to fall into place. The family's vines, which are in excellent condition, have won them a contract with the prestigious Torres wine company, which brings in vital money. The olive trees suffered terrible damage during a hard winter the year after the family moved to Spain but still manage to produce very high-quality oil. Although there is not much of it at present, it keeps them in stock for most of the year. Their almond trees are producing well and they are able to export nuts to England along with their recently launched Mother's Garden brand olive oil.

Integration has been surprisingly easy for them despite the language obstacles. Mac and Conxita are now considered their Catalonian family and Maggie and Martin are an integral part of village life. Martin has even taken a part-time job teaching English at the town hall. Ella and Joe Joe love their new life and friends, and they will both grow up healthy, happy and trilingual (English, Catalan and Castilian). Maggie too, although she still misses her friends and family, loves their new life and her garden is blooming and filling all their stomachs with healthy, home-grown food.

'It has taken us a while to figure it out,' admits Martin. 'We knew that the farm could make us some money but when we arrived we didn't know specifically how. Now we have a wine contract with Torres and we produce all our own olive oil as well as other things that allow us to cut our costs right back. We are also launching the Mother's Garden label under which we can sell and distribute produce from this area in the UK. We are not self-sufficient in the sense that we get everything we need from the farm. Of course we still have to visit the shops, and I do a lot of writing to supplement our income, but the farm allows us to be self-sufficient in the sense that we don't have to work for anyone else. This was what the dream was all about really: we are free to prioritise how we wish and to put far more energy into the family and enjoying this wonderful lifestyle. It is still hard work but we wouldn't want it any other way. For me personally the move has been everything that I hoped it would be . . . I spend twenty-seven hours more per week with Ella then I did before . . . and I've never felt better.'

Martin Kirby has written his own book about his family's move to Spain and it is entitled *No Going Back – Journey to Mother's Garden*. It is published by Time Warner Paperbacks and costs £6.99.

Martin also writes a monthly column about his new life in the Saturday sections of the *Eastern Daily Press* and *Yorkshire Post*.

For more information on the Mother's Garden label and for product lists and stockists, visit www.mothersgarden.org.

Top Tips

Martin Kirby offers some advice to others thinking of making a similar leap:

- First, however English-dominated the community is that you have set your heart on, commit yourself to learning the language. It will oil the wheels in so many ways, not least your understanding of a radically different bureaucracy that can become, if you find it hard to shake off the urgency and efficiency of life in Britain, a quicksand of frustration and confusion. You will also earn the respect of the locals for trying and you can't put a value on that.

- A priority has to be building up a network of people you can rely on for sound advice in the early days, hopefully long before you buy. Allow yourself time to research and make contacts.

- Applying for residency, making contacts and understanding fully how the system and society works – from house purchase legalities to medical services, opening bank accounts and finding craftsmen you can trust – all take up a huge amount of time, and you will have to bulldoze your way through some serious paperwork. Some people say that if you are in an empty waiting room you are in the wrong room. Steel yourself and be patient.

- We would also strongly urge that you read from cover to cover one of the several books about buying abroad before committing yourself. You need to discipline yourself not to be blinkered by the beauty of a property or its breathtaking position. If it doesn't have essential services, such as telephone or electricity, be clear on what the potentially high costs of acquiring them may be and be prepared to wait. Be realistic, too, about all costs, because taxes and fees can really add to what appears to be a giveaway price for a little piece of paradise.

- For people with children things like schooling, health and generally getting the family settled are bound to be major worries. But they might not be a problem if you find the right location close to a good community. In Catalonia they believe in keeping village schools going until the pupil number drops to about six or seven, so you may not have to look too far to find one. We have to fund books (just under a hundred Euros per child last year) and meet the cost of things like outings, but otherwise it is free.

- One more note of caution. Despite all the many new friends we have made here, one of the sternest tests remains the miles between us and our families and close friends in Britain (eased somewhat, it has to be said, by low-cost flights from Catalonia). It is one of the things that you may not put a high enough value on in the heady days of planning a new life abroad. I don't mean to be bleak, just realistic. It is a big step and, like the world over, there are pitfalls and people waiting to fleece you. If you do your homework, don't rush blindly into anything, and accept that it will take time to adjust and find your feet, you are well set to discover the happiness and adventure you seek.

Budget Sheet

How Martin and Maggie funded their move:

After paying for everything Martin and Maggie were left with a total of £20,000 to cover the cost of the move itself and to carry out the essential work required on the house at Mother's Garden. Martin estimates that by the time they arrived at their new home in Catalonia, the family had only £10,000 left to live on. This also had to cover the purchase of various machines to help them work the farm and, of course, Martin's trips back to the UK to visit his sick mother.

The family were able to supplement their income through crops grown on the farm, Martin's part-time teaching job and also his freelance journalism work. These sources, along with the publication in 2003 of his book *No Going Back – Journey to Mother's Garden* (Time Warner Paperbacks), have continued to pay for the gradual renovation of the house and adjacent guest house.

Martin is now working on a novel while continuing to write for newspapers and magazines. And he and Maggie are also beginning a new venture – exporting top-quality olive oil and possibly other local produce to Britain under their own Mother's Garden label. To find out more about Martin and Maggie, see www.mothersgarden.org.

Practical Directory – Catalonia

Region

Nestled in Spain's north-east corner and bordered by the Mediterranean on one side and the Pyrenees on the other lies the area of Catalonia. Famed for its striking diversity, the region boasts beautiful remote valleys, rugged mountains, lively coastal resorts, sleepy fishing villages and, of course, the cosmopolitan metropolis of Barcelona. The coastline is known as the Costa Daurada or Golden Coast, which, even with today's onslaught of north European and British home-buyers, remains predominantly Spanish.

Culture

Catalans are known to be fiercely patriotic, and the language issue has caused a rift between Barcelona and Madrid for years. A grasp of the Catalan language (*Català*) is an important starting point for anyone wishing to live here and almost essential if you want to work in business or the public sector.

The other thing that Catalans take very seriously is their food, with Catalan cuisine ranking with some of the best in all of Spain. *Sofregit* (tomato and onion fried in olive oil) and the quintessentially Catalan *samfaina* (a tasty combination of aubergines, peppers, onion, tomatoes and garlic) serve as the basis for many meals, while specialities of the region include *cargols* (snails), which are often stewed with rabbit and chilli.

Transport

Cheap flights to Barcelona, Gerona and Reus mean reaching

Credit	Value (£s)
Sale of Norfolk cottage	195,000
Total	**195,000**

the area from the UK is no problem. Avro operate low-cost flights to all three airports from many UK destinations, including London Gatwick, Manchester and Birmingham. For details see http://www.avro.co.uk or call 0870 458 2841. BA also fly to Gerona from London airports: see http://www.ba.com or call 0845 773 3377.

The *trens regionals* (regional trains) provide a good network across Catalonia itself. The *Catalunya Expres* from Barcelona is speedy but makes only limited stops, while fares can be around 15 per cent higher than other services. Delta trains only offer second-class travel but stop more often, while the Regional, again just second-class, stops everywhere. Where possible buy tickets for travel at the station before boarding your train.

Jobs

Unemployment figures in Catalonia are slightly below those recorded for the rest of Spain. Tourism is increasing in the area and providing jobs in all associated industries. There is also a demand for education monitors, social workers,

Debit	Value (£s)	Value (Euros)
Mortgage to be paid off on Norfolk cottage	70,000	104,448
Cost of buying Mother's Garden	95,000	141,933
Associated legal fees	7,000	10,458
Total	172,000	256,839

administrative workers, shop cashiers and bricklayers in the region. Surplus to requirements are accounting clerks, secretaries and construction painters.

Recruitment
The system for finding work in Spain is very similar to that of most EU member states. For a comprehensive guide to living and working in Spain you can visit the Jobcentre Plus website (http://www.jobcentreplus.gov.uk) following links through 'Looking for a job'> 'Working or training in Europe' > 'Spain'. Jobcentre Plus is part of a network of Public Employment Services that belongs to the EURES system (European Employment Services). EURES is a partnership of the European Economic Area (EEA) countries that exchanges information on vacancies and living and working conditions within the union. Throughout the EEA there are around 500 specially trained EURES advisors on hand to help you with queries; those in the UK can be contacted through your local Jobcentre Plus office. The website (http://www.europa.eu.int) contains listings with job vacancies from all over Spain. Both

EURES and Jobcentre Plus can also offer you help and advice on CVs, applications and vacancy listings. For more information you can call Jobseeker Direct on +44 (0)845 606 0234.

The Spanish equivalent of Jobcentre Plus is *Oficinas de Empleo* and any EEA member may use their services. They are run by the state *Instituto Nacional de Empleo* (INEM) and your local branch can be looked up via the website http://www.inem.es or in *la Guía Telefónica*.

Of course, there are alternatives to the state-run employment services – in Spain Private Placement Agencies exist and there are also temporary employment agencies (*Empresas de Trabajo Temporal*). Both types of agencies are run in a similar way to their UK counterparts and can be found in the Yellow Pages (*Páginas Amarillas*). The national press is also a good place to look for jobs. Papers such as *El Pais* and *El Mundo* carry heavy recruitment sections in their Sunday editions, although vacancies are also advertised in most daily editions. Regional papers often have recruitment sections too.

If you have a particular profession in mind and you want to find out more information on particular companies, it would be worth contacting both the Spanish and British Chambers of Commerce. Their contact details are as follows:

The Spanish Chamber of Commerce
126 Wigmore Street
London
W1U 3RZ
Tel: +44 (0) 20 7009 9070

Fax: +44 (0) 20 7009 9088
Website: http://www.spanishchamber.co.uk
Email: info@spanishchamber.co.uk

*Consejo Superior de las Cámaras Oficiales de Comercio
Industría y Navegación*
Diagonal 452
3a Planta
08006 Barcelona

Alcalá 99
60F
28009 Madrid
Website: http://www.camerdata.es
Email: informacion@camerdata.es

House Prices

Though not as pricey as the Costas del Sol and Blanca, the Costa Daurada still claims a premium on property simply by virtue of its being close to the Mediterranean. A coastal two-bedroom apartment, for example, is likely to set you back around £85,000 (€127,000), while a brand-new three-bedroom villa might cost £140,000 (€209,000). Property values here have risen steadily and are likely to continue to do so, however.

In line with the universal rule of the Spanish property market, inland properties will be cheaper than their coastal equivalent. Around £30,000 (€44,000) should secure purchasers a couple of hectares of land and a run-down house in need of almost complete renovation, while £65,000 (€97,000) could get you a property in good

condition with up to five hectares. Upwards of £100,000 (€149,000) buyers will be looking at large farmhouses in need of some work but with plenty of land and possibly even a pool. Again, increasing demand is pushing up prices steadily.

Tax

Since 1978 the Spanish state has been divided into seventeen Autonomous Communities, each with its own regional Government and Parliament. This means that taxation varies from one state to another but, broadly speaking, people living in Spain will be subject to the following taxation:

- Personal income tax on all income and earnings on capital they receive, irrespective of where the monies originated. The current rate stands at 33 per cent. European Union members have signed double taxation treaties, meaning that you will only be taxed once on income from any of these countries. The Spanish tax year coincides with the calendar year. Tax is applied progressively: the greater your taxable income, the greater your tax bill.

- Corporation Tax on taxable income received by legal entities such as companies or associations. The current rate stands at 35 per cent.

- Wealth Tax if the net worth of all their assets exceeds a minimum amount. The rate is progressive.

- Inheritance and Gift Tax on bequests and gifts *inter vivos*.

- Withholding Tax on particular types of income, such as income from non-property investments.

- VAT (value added tax) on the supply of goods and services by employers and professionals and on imports of goods.

- Excise duties on the consumption of certain goods such as alcohol and tobacco. The current rate is 40 per cent.

- Tax on capital transfers and documented legal acts. This is charged on legal and commercial documents and particular transactions, such as the purchase of fixed assets and the establishment of mortgages.

- Municipalities will also charge various local taxes such as real estate, business and car tax. These will vary regionally.

Residency

Nationals of European Union member states may live and work in Spain for up to three months without a residence permit providing they hold a valid identity document or national passport. If you are planning on staying longer than this you will need to visit your local police station or foreign office and obtain your residence permit (*tarjeta de residencia*). This will just be a formality as all EU members are entitled to the same rights, but the infamous Spanish bureaucracy will usually ensure a lot of legwork is involved. It is best to check before you visit exactly what documentation and photographs will be required by your local office for the Residence Card. Martin Kirby managed to fall foul of the system when he went to get Joe Joe registered. In an effort to get his young son to look at the camera, Martin was captured in the background of the photo – the Spanish authorities found this unacceptable and demanded a replacement picture.

All of the queues, paperwork and time involved in sorting out any administrative issues in Spain (including the residence permit) have given rise to a unique profession: that of the *gestor*. A *gestor* can be paid to sort everything out for you, and listings of *gestorias* can be found in the Yellow Pages (*Páginas Amarillas*). Prices vary considerably, so if you are going to take this short cut be sure to shop around. For further information contact the Ministry of Interior on 900 150 000 (toll free) from within Spain, or, if calling from abroad, on +34 (0) 91 537 24 23.

Other Registration Procedures

BRITISH CONSULATE

It is also a good idea to register your arrival and current address in Spain with the British Consulate. These can be located in all major cities.

FOREIGNER'S IDENTIFICATION NUMBER

This is your own unique identification number that will be used on much of the economic and professional paperwork that you will accrue while living in Spain. In order to obtain your NIE (*número de indentificación de extranjero*), you will need to visit the local *Oficina de Extranjero* (Office for Foreign Nationals) and present them with a filled-out application form, the original and a photocopy of your identification document or passport and documentation certifying the reasons or needs for your claiming an NIE.

SOCIAL SECURITY CARD

Before you begin working in Spain, you will need to obtain your social security membership number. You must provide a filled-in application form (TA –1) and your identity document in order to be presented with the social security card (*cartilla de seguridad social*). Once you have your number you can go to the corresponding health centre, where you will be assigned a doctor.

REGISTRATION

Although not a legal necessity, you may wish to register that you live in Spain. In order to do this, you need to pay a visit to your local *Ayuntamiento* (Council) to show them your accommodation rental contract or a utility bill with your address on.

Education

There is a publicly owned, free education system available to all children living in Spain. Many local schools are accountable to the Autonomous Community in which they are located so curricula may vary slightly. In addition there are also state-subsidised schools that satisfy requirements enabling them to receive some funding from the national government. These are also free to attend, though some charge small fees to cover academic materials. Should you wish your child to follow a British curriculum and/or be taught in English you will need to investigate international schools or privately owned schools of which there are plenty in Spain. The fees for these types of schools vary but are generally far lower than those paid in the UK.

Education is compulsory in Spain from the ages of six to

sixteen. After this the child may continue for an additional two or three years and study for their *Bachillerato* (school-leaving certificate). Pre-school education is not compulsory in Spain and provision varies from region to region, although the government must guarantee the existence of a sufficient number of places in order to provide schooling for those who request it. Most primary schools will have an infants' section for children between three and six years. Even in his remote corner of Catalonia, Martin was able to find pre-school education for Ella and Joe Joe which was provided by their local village school.

The school year follows broadly the same pattern as that of the UK, beginning in September. It usually finishes in June and children enjoy summer holidays of up to three months. Applications are generally submitted by April with enrolment formalised in June. In order to make your application you will need to take your identity documents to the relevant school. These include your passport and some proof of address – usually a bill will suffice. In addition, you will be required to show your child's birth certificate, photos (for identity purposes) and immunisation records. For older children you may also need school reports and proof of qualifications, which may need to be translated into the regional language. Again, as provisions and requirements vary from region to region, check with the town hall or the school itself.

Spanish universities are independent bodies and have the capacity to establish their own education provision. Students can study in whichever public university they wish, irrespective of their place of origin. Both public and private institutions are available.

Health

The respective Autonomous Community governs the provision of health care although the National Health system also exists as a means of state guarantee of quality and quantity of care. Provided you are paying into the social security system and have a social security card (*cartilla de seguridad sociar*), all persons living in Spain are entitled to free medical care and hospital treatment. Contributions to the social security system are obligatory for all employed persons and are made monthly, usually through your employer.

In Spain, 40 per cent of medical treatment is private and if you would prefer to have private medical coverage it can be obtained through one of the numerous health-care companies in Spain. These are best located through the Yellow Pages (*Paginas Amarillas*).

Useful Contacts

For more information on any aspect of living and working abroad visit the European Union website http://www.europa.eu.int. There is also a freephone helpline number: 00800 4080 4080.

CHAPTER 2

From London to the Chamonix Valley

When Debbie Flaherty and Alastair Johnston met and fell in love they instinctively knew that this relationship was going to be different from all the others that either had experienced in their lifetime. What they couldn't have known is that it would take them to the French Alps.

Life was good for Debbie and Alastair even while they were still London singletons. Debbie had lots of friends, a good income, her own house and was working as a human resources manager for the BBC. Alastair had a hectic social life as well, regularly indulging in his two primary passions – golf and skiing. He too owned a house and enjoyed a well-paid job as a supermarket store manager. And life only got better when the two were introduced by mutual friends, fell head over heels in love and embarked on a truly whirlwind romance.

'Less than a year after we met we were looking to buy a business together,' smiles Debbie. 'Our decision to pack it all in and move abroad was nothing to do with disillusionment about our lives in England – we were both enjoying London life enormously. The move was more related to the fact that it had taken me so long to finally meet the right person, I couldn't help thinking that it would be great to do something that allowed us to spend all our time together. We both felt positive about working as a team and being our own bosses.'

'The main catalyst for change was undoubtedly Debbie and I meeting,' agrees Alastair. 'There was no way I would have made any similar sort of move on my own; together it was our big chance. There was also just no reason not to do it: neither of us had any ties and the UK housing market had been kind to us both – it was a perfect time to sell up.'

In early 2001, the couple decided to take a holiday together and, as they both loved life on the piste, they decided that a week's skiing would be the perfect break. Alastair had been skiing since he was seventeen and was very keen to try the daunting Valley Blanche, near Mont Blanc in France – a twenty-two-kilometre off-piste ski run descending from the highest cable car in Europe; Debbie had never been to this region either and happily agreed to make it their destination; and so the couple booked a chalet in nearby Chamonix.

It was while they were excitedly making plans for their holiday that Alastair mentioned that a few years previously he had briefly held a fleeting dream to run a ski chalet and that, despite a lack of funds and partner, he had even got as far as making enquiries about the business and some properties.

Debbie was bowled over. 'God, I'd love to do that. What's stopping us now, why don't we actually do it?' she enthused.

As a passionate skier, Alastair didn't need much persuading – the dream was quickly rekindled and more solid plans built upon it.

The couple's first job was to make contact with agents in Chamonix ahead of their arrival and to view a few properties in between their quality time on the piste.

'We really just planned to get a feel for the industry,' admits Debbie. 'We thought we could price up a few places, look at how they are kitted out and what running a chalet would involve. We only had a couple of weeks before we set off but we managed to arrange to see a few potentials.'

Despite a propensity towards spontaneity, Debbie and Alastair put some thought into what sort of property they would want before contacting the agents. On the back of a cigarette packet they calculated that in order to make enough profit to live on, even in a bad season, they would need a minimum of six double rooms. In turn, this meant they also needed space for six en-suite bathrooms and a lounge, kitchen and dining room large enough to cater for twelve guests. They also wanted to live in their chalet, so they required sufficient space for their own living quarters – a garden and good view would be considered a bonus. The other key criteria was the property's position: it had to be fairly central and easy for people to get to; it also needed to provide easy access to the ski lifts.

It wasn't long after their touchdown at Geneva Airport that Debbie and Alastair realised that Chamonix was the perfect place for them to live and work.

'We drove from the airport and arrived in Chamonix at about three in the morning,' recalls Alastair. 'The first thing that struck us was how easy it was to get there from the airport: it was a very straightforward drive, no twisty little mountain roads – really accessible for tourists. The second thing was the atmosphere. Tired and disoriented, we ended up driving down Chamonix's main street the wrong way. It was mid-March, the middle of the night and it was chucking it down with snow, but the streets were packed with people out having a good time. It was a favourable first impression and made such a big impact on us that it didn't even matter that the following morning when we woke up all the snow had gone and it was raining!'

In between their long hours on the slopes, the couple trawled around properties and did a bit more homework about Chamonix. Everything they found out seemed to confirm their gut feeling that this was the place they should set up business.

'Commercially Chamonix made sense too,' Alastair continues. 'It has a really busy summer season which brings in lots of tourists as well as the skiing in the winter. House prices were pretty much going through the roof so we knew a property would be a great investment whatever we did with it. We also learned that easyJet were about to do more flights to Geneva.'

Alastair and Debbie didn't need much more convincing of Chamonix's merits and by the time they returned to London at the end of their week's skiing the pair were the proud owners of a large, though dilapidated, property there.

It was only when they returned to France a month later to meet some architects who were going to have a look at their wreck and offer opinions and costings on the transformation that Debbie and Alastair began to wonder what exactly they had let themselves in for. 'It really was a case of, "Oh God, what have we done?"' Alastair admits. 'The house was in a terrible position next to a main road and a railway line and needed an awful lot of work.'

Having paid a deposit, there would normally have been no get-out clause for Debbie and Alastair but, as luck would have it, a compulsory purchase order took the couple's problem house off their hands. It was to be flattened to build a roundabout, by order of the mayor. 'We were damn lucky to get out of that one,' Alastair smiles.

As they were still over in Chamonix, and not being the kind of people to let this setback dampen their enthusiasm, Debbie and Alastair decided to continue their search for a property in Chamonix. Unbelievably, they found one. Having arrived back in Chamonix owning one property, they now left owning a different one. The second property was a far better business proposition, the couple reasoned. It was in a good position and was certainly big enough to cater for their guests, though it did need a lot of costly work. However, by far the biggest problem with it from Debbie and Alastair's perspective was the fact that it was inhabited by tenants.

'Tenants have all kinds of rights under French law,' explains Debbie. 'We weren't allowed to evict them between November and April, in winter time. After five long months of negotiation with the property's occupiers, it became apparent they weren't going to leave. Fortunately one of the clauses in our contract for the property was that if we were unable to remove the tenants we could back out of the sale, which is what we had to do.'

Even with two unsuccessful house-buying attempts behind them, Debbie and Alastair did not allow themselves to be put off.

'I think by this point we had decided that we were going to do it one way or another,' comments Alastair. 'These were just minor obstacles that had to be dealt with. You never expect things to go smoothly; nothing happens that easily, that quickly. To be honest I think we probably assumed things would go wrong, but in our hearts we knew we would eventually find somewhere. Whatever country you are in, things rarely go right first time when you are buying a property.'

'We were using the services of a French-speaking solicitor based in London,' explains Debbie. 'So even though it might have seemed like we were being a bit reckless signing and leaving deposits in a country where we didn't speak the language or fully understand the intricacies of the property market, we always had good advice and our backs were covered legally speaking.'

'I think in a way our ignorance and the fact that we didn't know about all the pitfalls and bureaucracy associated with buying property in France helped us carry on undeterred,' Alastair adds. 'We hadn't done too much research so we were blissfully unaware!'

By this time they had made three trips to Chamonix and, still without a property, they decided that a fourth house-hunting trip was required, so in September they set off. Feeling that they were learning more with every chapter of their attempts to buy a chalet, when Debbie and Alastair saw a property that fitted almost all of their criteria, they once again had no hesitation in signing up for it.

It was a vast house that had been converted into three apartments and occupied a wonderful position near the town centre. Although its shell was sound and would remain untouched by its new owners, the property needed lots of work in order to become Debbie and Alastair's luxury chalet. The three apartments had to be converted back into a single house, which, in turn, needed to be divided into eight en-suite bedrooms and living quarters – this meant moving almost every interior wall. It also needed replumbing, rewiring, new windows and a complete interior overhaul. The couple waded in with an offer of €566,675 (£385,000), leaving them €147,000 (£100,000) in the kitty for the work. Their offer was accepted and this one was to take them all the way.

Back in the UK, Debbie's Wimbledon des res had been put on the market after their initial trip to Chamonix in March and had sold without a hitch for £250,000. She and Alastair were now living in his house, which was also on the market but proving a little more difficult to shift.

'When we signed for the first property in France I had gone to an agent and said I had a property I would like to put on the market,' he explains. 'She came round to look at it and then got terribly excited, saying she knew exactly who would buy it as he was looking for exactly this sort of home. Sure enough she contacted the guy and he said he'd take it, so it was never actually put out onto the general market. It all seemed too good to be true from my point of view . . . and sure enough it was! After two months he withdrew his offer because he couldn't sell his own property.'

When Alastair's canalside townhouse did finally get out

onto the general market there were plenty of people viewing but nobody actually wanted to buy it. Unbelievably it still hadn't sold by the time the deadline came for them to sign for the Chamonix property, on Boxing Day 2002, six months later. To make good the rest of the money owed on their French property, the couple had to take out a costly three-month bridging loan until Alastair's London house finally sold in March 2002.

With the final bit of capital needed for the move finally under their belts, Debbie and Alastair could really get things moving full steam ahead. The builders got started on the formidable task of transforming the chalet on 1 April, and the happy couple planned their final UK task – their wedding!

It was a wonderful day and the perfect chance to say goodbye to their much loved, and soon to be much missed, friends and family. But by far the best thing of all was that Mr and Mrs Johnston would be able to spend the rest of their lives on their honeymoon – a skiing trip to Chamonix!

D-Day was 1 July 2002. Having been assured by their architect that the work on the property was completed, the newly-weds gave up their jobs and headed to Chamonix to begin their new life. In high spirits they arrived at the chalet and rushed to inspect the transformation. They were met with what amounted to a building site – much of the structural work had been completed but there was no water or electricity, and it was clear that there was still an awful lot of work to do.

'It was quite frustrating,' sighs Debbie. 'Had we known it wasn't finished we would have stayed in our jobs longer and delayed coming out here. It wasn't anyone's fault though: what it came down to was a lack of communication between ourselves and our architect. Pascal – the builder – had informed her about the delay.

'We stayed in one of the rooms because it had been connected to the water mains but we lived without electricity for the next two weeks. Fortunately, as it was summer, this didn't matter too much; we hadn't planned or budgeted to be open for the summer season, so there was no rush.'

While Pascal and his team continued their work, Alastair and Debbie got on with theirs. There were eight rooms to furnish, towels, bed linen and crockery to buy, a web site to get online and a whole lot of marketing strategies to think through. The couple's first priority was to get Chalet Blanche on the tourist map so that potential customers would know it existed. This is easier said then done in Chamonix, where there are thousands of hotels and chalets offering similar services. The first port of call was local tour operators Big Foot and Up to You, who would include Chalet Blanche in their brochures and bring the punters in, but would take commission on every booking. In order to be put onto the tour operators' books, Chalet Blanche had to be vetted to check it was suitable. To Debbie and Alastair's delight it sailed through the inspection, confirming their hopes that it would be a top-quality venture.

There was also an awful lot of French bureaucracy to take on and, without speaking the language, this proved an almighty challenge.

'Dealing with a system you are not familiar with and without the language skills was a real problem,' admits Debbie. 'French Telecom hadn't connected our phone line and getting them to do it proved a nightmare. Trying to find out how to do things was difficult too. We got lots of conflicting advice on issues like whether or not we needed a licence to serve alcohol, and how we should register our business. Even when we tried to get French residency we were told different things. It was strange because everyone we spoke to gave us different information. We managed to get through it by talking to other English people here who had done it all before, but there was also a huge amount of trial and error involved. We had a French accountant who set up the business properly for us – this helped enormously.'

Despite running slightly behind schedule, Debbie and Alastair were delighted with the work Pascal and his team had carried out. By November the transformation of Chalet Blanche was complete and the quality of the work was flawless.

'We got a genuine bargain as far as the building work goes,' grins Alastair. 'People can't believe it when we tell them how much it cost: they'd reckon on it costing over twice as much. We had to do some extra bits like repairs to the roof, but it all came in pretty much within our budget. With the place looking like a ski chalet we couldn't wait to get our first customers in.'

But that is exactly where the problem lay; the couple had had several bookings from the tour operators but nothing had come in independently. What they had on their books by November was far from satisfactory.

'The winter season runs from mid-December until late April,' explains Debbie. 'And we still didn't have crucial

periods like Christmas week booked up. After such an enormous financial outlay, it would have been really gratifying to
see a full sheet of bookings.'

In order to drum up more business, Debbie and Alastair
flew to Olympia to attend the Ski and Snowboard Show and
flog their wares. An exhausting three days of selling and an
out-and-out charm offensive had led to many queries but still
nothing solidly booked. The couple simply had to return to
Chamonix and keep their fingers crossed.

To keep themselves occupied and take the edge off their
nerves, the couple decided to invite some friends over for a
trial weekend. They wanted to test their skills as hosts as
well as prepare themselves for the more practical aspects
such as cooking and cleaning. And what a shock to the
system it was.

While Debbie took the guests out sightseeing, Alastair
prepared the promised four-course gourmet meal . . . disas-
trously. It took him all day and resulted in burnt vegetables
and an unrecognisable crème brulée. It began to dawn on the
Johnstons that running a top-class business, in a top-class
resort, was going to be extremely hard work. This inkling
was confirmed when their first booked guests arrived.

'It was a wonderful feeling to have the place full of
guests,' says Debbie. 'This is what it was all about after all,
and we were dying to see whether we could pull it off. It was
exciting, nerve-racking and an awful lot of work, cooking
and running round after people all day. Really it's like having
a constant dinner party for fourteen people! We quickly
realised that we would have to cut down on the amount of
time we spent socialising with our guests. At first we would
go out with them until all hours of the morning and have to

crawl out of bed the next day to make breakfast and begin the cleaning. It was just unsustainable, especially when you consider that the winter season is thirty weeks long! We'd have run ourselves into the ground. Now we only go out a couple of nights with our guests, we really enjoy being sociable but it just isn't compatible with what we have to do the next day!'

Since the cameras left the Johnstons, the whole operation at Chalet Blanche has become a lot more professional and the bookings have rolled in. During the first winter season the business did better than either of them had predicted, with the chalet full for 70 per cent of the time, though they both attribute that largely to the *No Going Back* programme which was aired in the UK in January 2003. The Easter season also surpassed their expectations in terms of bookings, and two successful years later the books are filling up for 2004. When all the sums are said and done the couple have made about three times more than they had worked out on the back of that cigarette packet.

'The vast majority of our guests are people who have seen the programme,' confesses Alastair, 'and we get lots of requests for crème brulée! We have guests for more of the year then we thought and so we haven't been able to get out skiing as much as we would have liked, but I'm certainly not going to complain about that. We do get all of October and November off as it is dead in Chamonix. We haven't actually had the confidence to say no to a booking yet, but ideally we would like to be able to close completely for certain off-peak times of the year.'

To help with their almighty workload, and as a reflection

of their success, Debbie and Alastair now have a cleaning person to help with the chores and once a week some friends of theirs come in and take care of the evening meal, giving the couple an extra night off every week. Time and effort has been shaved off their workload too just through practise.

'We are still learning,' admits Debbie. 'The learning curve has been huge, but we are definitely becoming more streamlined. Neither Alastair nor I are the most organised of people and so we rarely plan things. This means we used to overlap each other on some of the jobs we had to do and always ran the risk of missing something entirely. It is so different from a "proper" job where there are guidelines telling you what your role is – maybe I should have set Alastair some objectives or something! I think we have both learned what we are good at and so we have grown into our roles a bit more now, we play to our strengths so the overlapping doesn't happen as often. I tend to deal with marketing and bookings whereas Alastair is more involved in the cooking.'

Alastair agrees wholeheartedly. 'We have definitely got far more used to the whole set-up and have refined things enormously. We can now prepare the meal for fourteen people in two hours because we know what to do and we are well practised. Just like any job, it becomes a routine operation. We have learnt what we can cut out from the recipes – things that take hours but nobody really notices – and that makes us much more efficient.'

And it's not just the business that is going well. On a personal level Debbie and Alastair are still as happy and in love – if not more so – than when they first got married. 'We get on extremely well,' they admit. 'And even the stressful times haven't really put a strain on our relationship.' As testament to their happiness there is some wonderful news to end the story . . . the couple are expecting their first child at the end of the year.

'We never thought of ourselves as maternal or paternal people,' laughs Debbie, 'so this wasn't really part of the game plan, but we are delighted and very excited. Our previous London existence just wasn't one that children fitted into, but being here and seeing the environment our kids would grow up in has influenced the decision enormously. There are child-friendly amenities right on your doorstep, the health care is wonderful and, of course, they would grow up bilingual.'

The hunt is currently under way for a new property which will serve as the family home because the lack of privacy at the chalet will become more of an issue when their first child is born. Asking whether the couple have any regrets seems pointless.

'It's a beautiful setting, a wonderful lifestyle and we get paid to be here,' smiles Alastair. 'It is very hard to think of a downside.'

For more details about Chalet Blanche see
http://www.demipiste.com or phone +33 609916018.

Top Tips

Debbie and Alastair offer some advice:
- The general work ethic in France takes some getting used to because it is so different from that in England. Even when the building work was running behind schedule our builders downed tools at precisely 12 noon

and took a two-and-a-half-hour lunch break. They weren't being lazy and we have absolutely no complaints about them, in fact we had a really good experience with our builders, but it does take some getting used to.

- While we were making efforts to buy a property in France we subscribed to several specialist magazines including *French Property News* and *Living in France*. We got a lot out of them because they are just full of letters and ideas from people doing the same thing. We found our architect and solicitor through contacts in the magazines.

- It is also really helpful to talk to local people about how to do things. We are very lucky because there are a lot of British people already living here and the employees of most service industries speak English. We made a very good contact early on through our estate agent – his name is Antoine and he just seems to know anybody who's anybody. He has helped us enormously.

- Persevere. When we came out on our first skiing holiday and were trying to make appointments with estate agents we found that they didn't really take us seriously. I guess they must get hundreds of Brits going to look at properties who don't actually buy or even have the intention of buying. It takes a long time before an agent will actually believe that you are serious – of the thirteen we had contact with, only one actually bothered to send us details of new properties when we were back in England. Demand here far outstrips supply so they don't worry too much about individual customers.

- Plan well ahead. Builders in Chamonix are like gold dust because there is so much building and construction work going on here. It is not unusual to have to wait months for builders to be able to start a job. They will come round and give you a quote and tell you that, yes, they are available, but when it actually comes down to it they can just pick and choose the jobs they want. We got our builders – who were excellent – through the aforementioned Antoine.

- Make sure that you have enough money if you are going to do it, and bear in mind that it always costs a lot more than you think it is going to. It is a good idea to have a contingency fund – and a fairly big one at that. Money just drains away very rapidly on living costs before you even have people coming to stay. It's unbelievable. You can never budget for everything – there is always a forgotten cost. Whatever budget you set for the amount of people you are going to get in, the difficulty is always getting punters in the door. Why should they come to you? There are thousands of other people doing the same thing.

- Consider how much you value your privacy and your own time. When you run a business like ours you are basically at the beck and call of your guests constantly, whether it is running them around in resort or trying to sort out ski hire. You won't get much privacy during the weeks when you have bookings.

- Learn how to cook, and learn the language. The biggest thing for us was not learning to speak French. It hasn't got in the way too much but it would be the biggest wish to improve on. We are taking French lessons now; they are going . . . I'm not sure how well!

Budget Sheet

How Debbie and Alastair funded their move:

Debbie and Alastair's business has been very successful over the past two years and both are delighted personally and financially. Based on the research they had done, the couple estimated that their potential turnover was £110,000 in the winter season (December to the end of April) and £40,000 in the summer season (May to the end of September). In their first year, they achieved 65 per cent of this turnover and in their second year they are set to achieve over 80 per cent. Thanks to the speed with which Chalet Blanche has taken off as a sought-after tourist destination, Debbie and Alastair are already beginning to recoup some of their massive outlay, as well as maintaining a comfortable lifestyle. They have been able to cut their annual marketing budget back to just £2000 thanks to the repeat bookings and personal recommendations that are filling their books.

The one financial hiccup in the couple's plans was Alastair's property not selling in time to complete on Chalet Blanche, and as a result the couple had to make use of a costly £200,000 bridging loan.

Practical Directory – Chamonix

Region

The Chamonix valley stretches some twenty kilometres and is tucked between the impressive Mont Blanc and Aiguilles Rouges mountain ranges. The area serves as a Mecca for outdoor enthusiasts both in summer and winter, offering mountaineering, hiking, climbing, biking and paragliding as well as world-class skiing. Chamonix itself sits at an altitude of around 1000 metres and is located in the north-westerly part of the Alps, just fifteen kilometres from both the Swiss and Italian borders. The town is situated at the foot of the highest peak in western Europe, Mont Blanc, which towers at an impressive 4808 metres. With a resident population of just 10,000 people, Chamonix town experiences a massive influx during the summer and winter tourist seasons when between 60,000 and 100,000 visitors arrive.

For more tourist information on Chamonix and the surrounding valley, try http://www.chamonix.net or http://www.chamonix.com – which lays claim to being the valley's official website.

Culture

Chamonix is a lively resort town for a large part of the year, only growing quiet in October/November and May, when most hoteliers and chalet owners take their own holidays. Of course the 'normal' community makes up the vast majority of the town's inhabitants, so at any time of the year there will be schools, hospitals, shops and supermarkets open as real life ticks on without the tourist influx.

Credit	Value (£s)
Equity released from sale of Wimbledon and Middlesex houses	300,000
Shares sold off annually to contribute to their current mortgage	15,000
Mortgage on French property	80,000
Savings	100,000
Total	**495,000**

In the winter season, skiers from all over the world descend upon the valley. They tend to be well-heeled and in their mid-twenties to forties, though Debbie and Alastair often have couples in their fifties staying with them. The après-ski in Chamonix made a huge impression on the couple when they first arrived; bars, restaurants and pubs line the streets and most nights are full of noisy but very good-natured holidaymakers. The summer season has a different feel, and though still lively and busy, the atmosphere is more relaxed with families and day trippers from Switzerland and Italy soaking up the sunshine and spectacular setting.

Transport

For Debbie and Alastair, part of the appeal of Chamonix is its accessibility. Local roads are excellent, and there is even direct autoroute (motorway) access to the town. Should you

Debit	Value (£s)	Value (Euros)
Cost of Chamonix chalet	385,000	566,675
Associated costs (including notaire's fees)	24,000	35,000
Renovation	100,000	147,000
Decoration and equipment	22,000	32,000
Marketing	15,000	22,000
Total	546,000	802,675

choose to take a ferry from the UK, the drive time from Calais to Chamonix will be around nine hours. When working out your budget, remember to factor in toll charges. There is also the option of the train network, which, again, is excellent in France. From the Eurostar stops in either Lille or Paris, French rail operators SNCF or TGV routes run to Chamonix, though you will have to change trains or complete the last part of the journey by car.

Having said this, air travel will nearly always be quicker and less expensive. The closest airport is Geneva (around one hour's drive from Chamonix), to which easyJet runs frequent and inexpensive flights from London, Liverpool and the East Midlands (http://www.easyjet.com). British Airways (http://www.britishairways.com) and Cross Air (http://www.swiss.com) also have lots of flights, so it might be worth looking out for cheap deals. Chambery and Lyon airports are also within a reasonable distance with transfer times of approximately one-and-a-half hours and two hours and forty-five minutes respectively.

Jobs

Chamonix is situated in the French region of the Rhône-Alpes which has a current unemployment rate of 8.3 per cent – 1 per cent lower than the French national average. However, the job market is suffering deterioration due to limited industrial growth throughout France.

Construction workers are currently in quite high demand (these include bricklayers, stonemasons, concrete placers and finishers, carpenters, joiners, plasterers and plumbers). Nurses too are sought after so keenly that they are being drafted in from Spain. As you might expect, the tourist trade is significant throughout the Rhône-Alpes and is still increasing apace. The hectic summer and winter tourist seasons bring in thousands of visitors requiring waiters, waitresses and bartenders. In 2002 some 20,000 jobs were advertised in this sector.

Recruitment

The system for finding work in France is very similar to that of most EU member states. For a comprehensive guide to living and working in France you can visit the Jobcentre Plus website (http://www.jobcentreplus.gov.uk) following links through 'Looking for a job'> 'Working or training in Europe' > 'France'. Jobcentre Plus is part of a network of Public Employment Services that belong to the EURES system (European Employment Services). EURES is a partnership of the European Economic Area (EEA) that exchanges information on vacancies and living and working conditions within the union. Throughout the EEA there are around 500 specially trained EURES advisors on hand to help you with queries; those in the UK can be contacted through your local Jobcentre Plus office. The website (http://www.europa.eu.int) contains listings with job vacancies from all over France. Both EURES and Jobcentre Plus can also offer you help and advice on CVs, applications and vacancy listings. For more information you can call Jobseeker Direct on +44 (0) 845 606 0234.

The *Agence Nationale pour Emploi (ANPE)* is the French equivalent of Jobcentre Plus. All EEA members can use its services, which include:

- Preliminary counselling

- Careers information

- Training scheme or job placement

- UK-style job clubs

An *ANPE* office can usually be found in major towns and cities and some offer specialised fields. For example, an *ANPE Cadres* deals with executive- or management-level recruitment, while in Paris some offices deal with professions such as catering or journalism. Your nearest branch can be found listed in the Yellow Pages (*Les Pages Jaunes*) or you can contact the Head Office:

ANPE
Immeuble Le Galilée
4 rue Galilée
93198 Noisy-le-Grand
Paris Cedex
Tel: +33 (1) 49 31 74 00
Fax: +33 (1) 43 05 67 86
Website: http://www.anpe.fr

Temping agencies work much the same way in France as in the UK. They are called *Agences de Travail Temporaire* and you will need your French social security number to register. To get this you should apply to your local *Caisse de Sécurité Sociale d'Assurance Maladie*. Well-known UK temping agencies such as Manpower, Bis and Ecco are major players in France too so it might well be worth a visit to your local branch before you depart.

French national papers such as *Le Monde*, *Le Figaro* and *France-Soir* will all contain job vacancy listings, while *Carrière et Emploi* is a magazine specifically for recruitment.

In addition to these avenues for finding work, there is a computer database system called *Minitel* which allows users access to all kinds of information including job vacancy listings. You can also advertise yourself as a jobseeker. The system is accessed through a special terminal by any subscriber to the French telecom system (*Agence commerciale des Télécommunications*).

For work directories and other useful pamphlets you can contact the cultural section of the French Embassy in London.

French Embassy
58 Knightsbridge
London
SW1X 7JT
Tel: +44 0870 005 6717
Fax: +44 (0) 20 7073 1004
Website: http://www.france.embassyhomepage.com

If you plan to be self-employed you will need to visit your local Department for Work and Pensions International Services (DWP) or search on their website http://www.dwp.gov.uk/international/sa29. Should you wish to set up your own business, contact the *Agence Nationale pour la Création d'Enterprise (ANCE)* in your region or contact the local Chamber of Commerce.

House Prices

House prices in Chamonix are increasing almost exponentially, buoyed by continued high demand, particularly from the British (according to estate agents Brits comprise around 70 per cent of people wishing to buy property in Chamonix). Within the last three years, it is estimated that property prices have increased by around 40 per cent; great news for anyone who already owns a property and can therefore sit back and watch their capital appreciation go through the roof, but it is potentially problematic for those not yet with a foot on the ski property ladder. And although new-build properties and residential developments are continually being constructed, there is still an overall deficit in properties.

You can expect to pay from around €295,000 (£200,000)

for a well-located two-bedroom apartment; top-specification new-build units will sell from around €413,000 (£280,000). The chances of finding a property of a similar size to Debbie and Alastair's – and in good condition – are fairly remote, but the goal is probably worth some exploratory legwork. Be sure to allow a budget of at least half a million pounds sterling, and remember that there will be hefty costs on top of this. In France, notaires' fees and property taxes can add 10 per cent on to the asking price.

Tax

French taxes are not deducted at source and instead, in February each year, taxpayers are asked to fill in a tax return (*declaration d'impôts*) to assess their annual income. Tax on this income will be payable the following year, either in ten monthly instalments or by payment three times a year. Tax returns are sent to your local *Centre de Paiement des Impôts*, whose address can be located at the town hall (*Mairie*). The tax levied on income is calculated based on the gross salary earned by a person or couple. This total is offset against various allowances according to the household's situation. The maximum income tax rate is 49.58 per cent.

Other taxes paid by French residents include:

- The RDS (Reimbursement of social debt) and the CSG (supplementary social security contribution in aid of the underprivileged). These levies contribute to the social security system and are based on income.

- Property taxes which are paid by the owner and are based on property type and locality

- Residence tax

- Audio-visual licence – annual fee if you have a television

- VAT (value added tax), the rate of which depends on the product type

For more information contact:

> Inland Revenue International Division (Double Taxation)
> Victory House
> 30–34 Kingsway
> London
> WC2B 6ES
> Tel: +44 (0) 20 7438 6622

The Inland Revenue website contains information on taxation and online versions of each of its forms: http://www.inlandrevenue.gov.uk

Residency

Nationals of European Union member states may live in France without a residence permit for up to three months, providing they hold a valid identity document or national passport. For stays of over three months in duration you will need to apply for an EU residence permit (*Carte de Séjour de Ressortissant de l'Union Européene*). These can be obtained from the police headquarters (*Préfécture de Police*), the local police station (*Commissariat de Police*) or town hall (*Mairie*).

You will need to take with you:

- a valid passport or identity card

- a *fiche d'état civil* (an original civil state paper such as a birth or marriage certificate)

- proof of address (such as utility bills or rent receipts)

- offer of employment/employment contract, or the necessary authorisations from the Chamber of Commerce in the case of self-employment or setting up a business (four copies are needed)

- three passport-size photos

Education

France offers a free state education to every child and schooling is compulsory between the ages of six to sixteen. In order to obtain a list of schools within your municipality, you will need to contact your local town hall. In order to register your child at any level of schooling you will first need to visit the town hall to obtain a registration certificate that will tell you which school to register your child in. If you are unhappy with the allocated school you can apply for a derogation which will allow you to choose the school.

You need to take the following with you to the town hall:

- your official family record book

- a document stating your child has had all the vaccinations necessary for his/her age group

- a declaration of residence

Your child's registration will be recorded by the headmaster at the appointed school when you produce:

- the registration certificate issued by the town hall

- the official family record book

- a certificate issued by your doctor confirming that the child is healthy and psychologically mature enough to attend school

- a certificate of vaccination

From the age of two, children can be sent to nursery school; they can stay there until September of the calendar year in which they have their sixth birthday. This cycle of education is not compulsory. If there is no nursery school in your municipality you can register your child at the infants section of the local primary school.

Compulsory education begins with the five years spent at primary school (*école primaire*), which is divided into the 11th to 7th forms. From here children go to secondary school (*école secondaire*) until they are fifteen; this stage is divided into 6th to 3rd forms. When they complete the 3rd form, children will attend high school (*lycée*), where they can specialise their studies and take the corresponding *baccalaureate* – a prerequisite for university entry.

There is also a private school system, which predominantly consists of Catholic schools. Some of these are supervised and part-funded by the Ministry of Education; those that are not rely on considerable fees. Private schools account for around 20 per cent of all secondary education.

There is also the choice of international schools of which there will be several in most major towns. For further information contact:

> European Council for International Schools
> 21 Lavant Street
> Petersfield
> Hampshire
> GU32 3EL
> Tel: +44 (0) 1730 268 244
> Fax: +44 (0) 1730 267 914
> Email: ecis@ecis.org
> Website: http://www.ecis.org

Higher education in France is admired worldwide for its quality and accessibility. Public institutions are completely subsidised by the Government and access is strictly by merit-based exam. For further information you can contact the Ministry of Education's information service:

> Office National d'Information sur les Enseignements et les Professions
> 12, Mail Barthélemy Thimonnier
> BP 86-Lognes
> 77423 Marne-la-vallée
> Cedex
> France
> Tel: +33 (1) 64 80 35 00
> Fax: +33 (1) 64 80 35 01
> Website: http://www.onisep.fr

Health

The health-care system in France is complex and provided for by a whole host of public and private sector institutions. It is paid for primarily through the income-related CSG welfare levy, though other taxes on companies and workers contribute. French social security cover is generally only partial and for this reason many people also subscribe to non-profit health insurance cooperatives known as *mutuelles*. Standard procedure is to take your *feuille de soins* (a statement of treatment provided by the doctor) and *vignettes* (the detachable stamps in prescription packaging denoting the price of the medication) to the *Caisse de Securité Sociale* (Social Security office) for partial reimbursement. The address of your nearest office can be obtained from the local town hall.

Only visits to doctors and dentists working within the French sickness insurance scheme (*Conventionnés*) are partially reimbursed by sickness insurance. The French health-care system is currently under review and reforms are expected in the near future.

Useful Contacts

Much of the information on these pages has come from EURES – the European Job Mobility Portal. For more information on any aspect of living and working abroad visit their website at http://www.europa.eu.int. There is also a freephone helpline number: 00800 4080 4080.

A lot of information was also provided by Jobcentre Plus, who are part of the EURES network. For more information visit www.jobcentreplus.gov.uk or call Jobseekers Direct on +44 (0) 845 606 0234.

Other information was supplied by the French property agents:

VEF (UK) Ltd
4 Raleigh House
Admirals Way
London
E14 9SN
Tel: +44 (0) 20 7515 8660
Fax: +44 (0) 20 7515 5070
Email: info@vefuk.com
Website: http://www.vefuk.com

The website http://www.moving-to-france-made-easy.com is also very useful.

CHAPTER 3

From Maidstone to the Salzkammergut

Darron Day and wife Lesley uprooted themselves and their children Katy (thirteen) and Chris (eleven) from Maidstone in Kent to a sleepy Austrian village called Obertraun. Their plan is to set up a hotel there, and although the project is taking shape well with no major mishap or catastrophe, settling the children down to their new lives is proving difficult.

Darron, gregarious and affable, used to work as a milkman. 'I would sometimes work 85 hours in one week,' he says. 'I enjoyed it enormously but the hours were taking their toll and after sixteen years I felt it was time for a change.'

The decision wasn't taken lightly by Darron as there were aspects of the work that he really enjoyed. He was so popular that several of his clients nominated him for an MBE, which he was duly awarded in June 1999.

'Most days I would have to get up at around 1.30 a.m.

and I'd be delivering till 9 or 10 a.m. the following morning. I was getting very little sleep, quite often just three hours or so. On Saturday nights I was able to get maybe seven or eight hours, but I always had a headache on Sunday because my body wasn't used to it.

'My contract with Unigate was renewed on a three-year basis and after thirteen years I decided to renew it just one more time. This would give us three years to think about what we were going to do.'

For Lesley life had been much simpler: 'I was doing some hairdressing, and some cleaning for a few friends, but nothing stressful. I only had to make enough money to look after the horses. Apart from that I just rode them and looked after the kids. The move was certainly not about eliminating stress from my life. I was interested in trying something different, though.'

Darron had always held a dream of opening a bed-and-breakfast. When he and Lesley met they had both been working in the catering business – he was a chef and she a waitress. When discussions began about what change of direction the family could undertake, this seemed the obvious choice. 'My ideal move would have been to the New Forest,' admits Lesley, 'but the property prices were just too expensive. There is no way we could have bought something big enough to do what we wanted to do. We also looked at Wales and Cornwall with the idea of opening a campsite or caravan park – I wanted to explore everything in the UK before contemplating anything abroad, although Darron was keen to move overseas from the word go.'

*

With the UK property market throwing up altogether prohibitive prices, Lesley agreed with Darron that the move should be abroad and suggested Austria. The family had been holidaying there for many years and loved the country.

'Portugal would have been the obvious choice because I was brought up there,' says Lesley. 'I know everything about the place and my father had left my brother and me a property there in his will. But for me, our new home had to be a place with seasons. I wanted greenery and a clean, fairly westernised country. We started looking in France because the property prices are so low, but our love of Austria, and the realisation that we could easily run a bed-and-breakfast there, won out in the end.'

With the decision made, the Days turned to the Internet to help them with their search for Austrian property. Quite by accident they stumbled on a website run by English expatriate David Potter Euroburo Ltd. He lived and sold property in the Salzkammergut – a picturesque area of lakes and mountains bordering the Styria, Upper Austria and Salzburg provinces. The website was so comprehensive that Darron and Lesley made contact. They told David that they wanted to buy a property or business that they could run as a bed-and-breakfast and he was quick to assure them that he could provide them with plenty of options. With this in mind and given the fact that they found it difficult to access other Austrian property sites, the Days' search for a property began and ended in the Salzkammergut. They knew it was a beautiful part of Austria as they had driven through it themselves en route to skiing holidays in Tirol and Mayrhofen.

It wasn't long before Darron and Lesley were boarding a plane and making the trip to Austria to view some of David's properties. They looked at four altogether but there was something about the Seerose Hotel that really captured their imagination. It was located in the pretty village of Obertraun, amid the Dachstein mountains on the eastern shore of the Hallstätt lake – a spectacular location.

'The Seerose had been empty for ten years so it was quite run-down,' says Lesley. 'There was algae all over the outside and it was a lot bigger than we had initially wanted, but I could see the potential. It had a beautiful lakeside position and benefited from having two tourist seasons, one in winter and an even busier one in the summer. Money was quite a big part of the move for me,' she continues. 'I could see us making a very comfortable living and the property was an absolute bargain. It was a great opportunity.'

The Seerose Hotel, like most properties in Austria, had been handed down through a long family line and had only come onto the market due to the divorce of the couple who had previously owned it. They had spent a lot of money doing the property up and buying brand-new furniture. When they split up they also had to declare themselves bankrupt and so the bank repossessed the property.

The Seerose had a land value of €476,000 (£330,000). It also had a restaurant and kitchen, a bar and sufficient rooms to create eight spacious self-contained apartments, not to mention a wonderful lakeside position. The bank was simply trying to clear its debts, so the property was on the market for €325,000 (£225,000). The Days would happily have paid this sum but David assured them there was no need – as the place had been empty some ten years the price could be knocked down.

'Really he took it from there,' recalls Darron. 'We ended up getting the place for €190,000 (£133,000), a grand total of €221,000 (£152,000) including all transfer fees and legal costs – we couldn't believe our luck.'

And the good news just kept coming. All the furniture – enough to equip all eight apartments – had been included in the sale price as the bank had no need for it. When the packaging was removed, the Days were astounded to discover it was all Voglauer – the most expensive and sought-after brand of furniture in Austria. Their haul had an estimated value of €130,000 (£90,000)!

With the papers signed, Darron and Lesley rushed back to England to set their finances in order. Their five-bedroom house in Maidstone was on the market but wasn't selling – it coincided with a slump in the UK market and it just seemed that it couldn't be shifted. They found a buyer eventually but it was quite a tense time.

Once they had cashed in their two endowment policies and combined this with the money made from the sale of their house they were able to buy their Austrian property outright.

'Financially the Seerose Hotel has been a dream,' reflects Darron. 'And to be honest, that has been more through luck than judgement. There has been plenty of red tape to cut through but so far it has worked in our favour. We have also recently found out that we may be entitled to a grant for up to a quarter of the value of our property to help with the restoration. Our neighbour Michael is helping us pursue that line of enquiry.'

With their UK property finally sold it was time to start sorting through their belongings. They needed to pack up everything they were going to take with them to Austria and get rid of what they were leaving behind. Sadly for Lesley this included her two eldest sons from a previous marriage, Stuart (twenty-one) and Paul (twenty-three). Paul had moved out of the family home some months previously, but Stuart was finding life in the nest a little too comfortable to voluntarily make the same move.

'Darron and I are pretty liberal parents,' admits Lesley. 'Stuart was having a wonderful time: I fussed over him, he was able to have his girlfriend over whenever he wanted and we all got on famously. As he saw it, there was just no need to move out. When we sold the house I ended up having to almost forcibly remove him. It broke my heart as I didn't want to leave them behind but they both had their own lives. They are living together in Maidstone now and seem fairly settled.

'It's strange but aside from the boys I really wasn't sad to leave,' she muses. 'I thought I would be – we'd been in the house for seventeen years. Wherever we were going it was time to go.'

Darron and Lesley's children Katy (thirteen) and Chris (eleven) were to make the move to Austria with them. The flaw in this plan was that both were incredibly settled and happy with their Maidstone lives. Katy loved school and had some very close friends, while Chris was his local team's star footballer. In short, they did not want to leave.

In order to give the children a glimpse of their new life, Lesley and Darron flew them out in the summer to visit Obertraun.

'The place was buzzing and full of tourists,' enthuses Darron. 'It was about forty degrees and the beach on the edge of the lake was packed. There were people of all ages there.' This was very encouraging for Darron and Lesley, whose future income depended on the tourist trade in the area, but the best news was yet to come.

'Virtually every house in Obertraun offers bed-and-breakfast, or at least some form of accommodation, so we didn't think we would need to worry about booking somewhere for our overnight stay. However, a quick visit to the local tourist office led to the discovery that every room in Obertraun was taken, there was nowhere for us to stay. It was a slight inconvenience at the time,' smiles Darron, 'but a wonderful omen for our own future there.'

Katy and Chris were less impressed, however – the move still did not appeal to them.

Back in England, things began to seem a little more real . . . and a little more daunting.

'I think there comes a time for everyone who makes this sort of move where the realisation sets in,' admits Lesley. 'For the first couple of months there were just lots of "yes's". "Yes, we can really afford to do this. Yes, we can bring the dog and horses. Yes, we can get the kids into school." Then suddenly it hits you: wow, we are really doing this. The fluffy image of living on permanent holiday becomes reality and you realise there are going to be Monday mornings out there, and that when you get those inevitable problems they might be more difficult to sort out because of the language barrier.'

Nevertheless, the Days pushed ahead with their arrangements and before they knew it, it was time to say their farewells. After an emotional goodbye from her classmates, Katy now had to leave her beloved cat who was too old to make the move with them and was to be left with a relative. She was distraught.

The family drove themselves over to Austria, and the time spent in the car gave them all the chance to calm down and contemplate their new life. Katy and Chris, both upset, were told that the homesickness would pass and that in no time they would consider Austria as their home.

The family planned to live in the top apartment of the hotel which was being converted into living quarters, but as the Seerose was uninhabitable when they moved, they had arranged to stay in rented accommodation in nearby Bad Aussee. From here the kids could easily catch their train to school, while Darron and Lesley could get to Obertraun to begin work on the Seerose.

The problem of rent going out of the Days' account without anything coming in was circumvented by the desirability of their inherited furniture. Their landlord readily accepted a couple of pieces in exchange for the rent of his apartment for two months. The family were, at least, warm, cosy and in pocket.

Although the Seerose was structurally sound, it was basically just a shell and therefore a lot of cosmetic work had to be carried out before the place could be considered a home, much less a hotel. In addition to the family's living quarters, the building was to be converted into eight self-contained apartments, all of which needed bathrooms and kitchens. The restaurant and bar area also needed modernisation and the exterior needed a serious facelift before it could be expected to attract guests. To cover the costs, Darron had secured a loan from an Austrian bank for €200,000 (£140,000), so they had a year's grace before they had to start thinking about paying it back.

Having settled into their snug rented flat, the family trouped down to have a look at their hotel. For Lesley the reality of the Seerose that day presented a pretty grim picture. November was an altogether different experience from their previous summer visits. 'It was minus thirteen, the place had no heating, it was more run-down than I remembered and the whole task just seemed too big to contemplate,' she admits. 'Those first few weeks were incredibly hard for me: I really couldn't muster any vision or enthusiasm for the place. I would find that I just couldn't face coming down and seeing it, let alone helping Darron with any of the work. I used to go for long walks by myself and wonder what we had done.'

Lesley soon pulled herself together and once they, and their builders Gerhard and Helmut, had begun the work, things began to take shape remarkably quickly. 'There are several milestones we have passed that have felt like huge breakthroughs. Just getting the boiler clunking into action and getting some heat through the place made a world of difference – painting walls is a particularly dismal task if attempted in temperatures of minus ten! Painting the exterior was a big boost too – it made the place look so much more welcoming, and finishing the first apartment was a great day,' recalls Lesley. 'We have another English couple living there at the moment because the property they have just bought in the village is in a similar state to the Seerose two months ago!'

Despite their progress and the freedom from financial crisis, to say the transformation of the Seerose into self-catered accommodation was smooth would, of course, be wrong. Lesley found her experiences with the builders incredibly trying.

'Gerhard was very likeable but he clearly enjoyed talking more than working and I found his lack of progress astonishing at times. I waited weeks for him to lay my lounge floor but he always found things he felt he should do first. Somehow our vision never quite met in the middle!' she admits. 'They constantly left the place in a complete state too. Every time a room was finished I would tidy and clean it, and then shampoo the carpets. The following day I would find it filthy again as it was being used as a store room for some dirty parts or dusty furniture.

'I was frustrated too that I was always the bad guy. Darron is so chatty and friendly that he never shouted or nagged at Gerhard, that was always left to me. I became known by all as 'the chief' – an affectionate term, I'm sure!' she smiles.

The Days also changed their building plans slightly when Darron picked up a sauna at a bargain price in the sales. Now intent on installing a sauna and a playroom, two of the apartments were to be sacrificed and made into en-suite double bedrooms. 'Settling in and doing up the hotel was a stressful time, but to be honest it was no worse than we had anticipated,' says Darron. 'We always had our clean, warm flat to return to at the end of the day. Katy and Chris still moaned and used the move as ammunition sometimes, but they were better than we had thought they might be. They both got up and went to school in the morning with no more complaints than we ever experienced in Maidstone.'

Darren and Lesley began to integrate too. When they first arrived in Obertraun, they found they had a quasi-celebrity status within the small community. Everyone knew that 'English' people had moved into the Seerose and found the family a bit of a novelty. However, it wasn't long before Darron's outgoing nature and love of socialising had won the couple firm friends despite their shaky language skills. Within two months of living in Austria Darron also found himself enlisted into the local fire brigade, a definite confirmation that the family were now part of the community. While out with his friend and neighbour Hannes, whom he knew to be the chief of the Fire Service, he had mentioned that he might be interested in joining.

'The fire brigade is voluntary out here so I thought I'd make some enquiries,' laughs Darron. 'It's something I've always been interested in but I thought I would need some sort of qualification or training. In fact, the next night Hannes popped round to measure me up for my uniform . . . it was all very informal and quick.'

With work on the hotel running almost on schedule, the Days were able to move into their Seerose apartment before Christmas 2003, and with four of their apartments completed they were able to welcome their first paying guests over the New Year. 'It was very exciting,' says Darron. 'We were a bit nervous but the guests were all self-catered so we didn't have the added worry of providing food for them. Nine of them were Brits and fourteen were Austrian and all were in high festive spirits, which made it all very good fun.'

Darron and Lesley might have thought that by running at half capacity they were easing themselves gently into life as hoteliers, but as fate would have it disaster struck, which resulted in them both receiving a baptism of fire.

'At about 2.30 a.m. on New Year's Day the oil in the boiler ran out,' grimaces Darron. 'We had been assured that it would last until March so it was a terrible shock to suddenly discover we had no hot water, especially with twenty-three paying guests and a Bank Holiday the next day. After frantic telephone calls and visits we managed to locate some, but I ended up driving over 100 kilometres to the garage to collect it. I didn't get back till 8.30 a.m. and finally managed to get the boiler going again. The funniest thing about the story is that not a single one of our guests noticed! Thankfully a heady combination of Glühwein and apple strudel meant they had slept through the whole adventure.'

Despite the shaky start to 2004, the rest of the year to date has turned out extremely well for the Days. An opening party in February marked the official beginning of the Seerose Hotel's new lease of life and all the occupants of Obertraun were invited.

'We were helped tremendously by the locals here,' explains Darron. 'The people in Austria are so nice and we found ourselves with lots of support from the whole village. I think everyone was keen to see the Seerose open again.'

More details about the Seerose Hotel and the luxury apartments for rent within it can be found at http://www.darrondaymbe.com. For information by phone call +43 (0) 6131 26754.

Top Tips

Darron suggests:

- Learn the language. Although we had some lessons before arriving here it was nothing like enough. It is sometimes an unwelcome strain to try and relax with a drink but also have to conduct a conversation in an unfamiliar language, yet it appears rude if you make no effort. It is better to be comfortable with the language before being forced to use it.

- Make sure you make the effort to integrate. Even though we didn't know very much German, we were able to make some good friends over a glass or two of schnapps. Austrians are so friendly that this is easily done and definitely worth it. The locals have been so helpful to us and offered sound advice at difficult times. We wouldn't have found out that we might be entitled to a crucial loan had it not been for our neighbour.

- Use an agent. David made our lives so much easier and was on hand to answer all our questions and provide us with a range of properties to view when we made our trip over. This saved us valuable time. It also meant we never had to worry about all of the red tape involved when buying and he got us an excellent price because he was familiar with the local market.

David Potter (the agent used by the Days) of http://www.euroburolimited.co.uk has operated and lived in Austria for many years. He offers the following advice:

- There are lots and lots of banks in Austria and they usually operate at a regional level. This means that it is not unusual for your bank to be unheard of in another province. Before enrolling be sure to check out the fees involved in transferring or receiving money; they can be extortionate. It is also worth bearing in mind that there are no cheques here at all, and credit cards are not widely accepted. Most payments are done using a debit card or Bankomat.

- Although, as Britain is a member of the EEC, UK nationals can go to live and work in Austria without a residence permit, you are legally obliged to let the authorities know that you are there and where you are residing within three days of arrival. You will need to go to the Registration Office (*Meldeamt* – located either at the town hall or police station) with your passports.

- Among the straightforward questions on the Confirmation of Address form there is one that really threw me. You are asked what your religion is and given the two options, either Catholic or Evangelical. There is a Church Tax in existence in Austria and, although we have never received a bill for it, it is probably for this reason that you are asked. You may want to be prepared for this question if you plan to write something other than the two options listed on the form.

- If you are planning an evening dancing the night away at a nightclub, you might want to do some homework before deciding on a venue. Many 'nightclubs' are actually brothels, which are legal in Austria and, as it happens, a nice little tax earner for the government.

- Please think carefully about buying a house in mountain areas if you are not going to live there. The winters are harsh here with temperatures regularly falling to minus 20 or even minus 30, so unless you can afford to pay someone to regularly shovel the snow away, you may find your house rapidly becomes a glacier. If you only live in the house for part of the year you may also find you are liable for Tourist Tax.

- It is probably not worth bringing telephones, faxes or modems from the UK out to Austria with you. The telephone system here is operated by Telekom Austria and it is wired differently from those found in the UK. In spite of lengthy efforts, our Telecom engineer was unable to get any of our equipment working.

Budget Sheet

How Darron and Lesley funded their move:
The Days are the first to admit how lucky they have been financially in finding and securing the Seerose Hotel. They got an extremely good deal paying just £133,000 for a property with a land value exceeding £330,000 simply because it was being sold by the bank, not an agent or owner.

The Days had budgeted a spare €20,000 (£14,000) to cover living costs and the initial running costs of the hotel. Things have gone so well that Darron hopes to buy a

Credit	Value (£s)
Sale of five-bedroom Maidstone property	220,000
Austrian bank loan	140,000
Total	*360,000*

minibus out of this sum for his airport runs to and from Salzburg collecting guests. It also seems likely that the family will be eligible for the restoration grant that will reimburse them around a third of the cost of the work they did at the Seerose.

And not only was the property itself a bargain, the business looks set to boom too. 'It doesn't look like we're going to have any problems getting bookings,' smiles Darron. 'Unlike almost all the other hotels and accommodation in Obertraun, the Seerose is all newly kitted out and so it is widely considered the best. We have had enquiries from representatives of major football teams who train in the region in summer and the tourist board want to place their bookings with us too. The future is definitely looking bright!'

Debit	Value (£s)	Value (Euros)
Cost of Seerose hotel	120,000	170,000
Cost of furniture	13,000	20,000
Associated purchase costs	20,000	29,000
Labour	97,000	140,000
Decoration and equipment	27,000	40,000
Total	**277,000**	**399,000**

Practical Directory – Austria

Region

Although the Days live close to Salzburg, their village – Obertraun – actually lies within the borders of the province of Upper Austria (*Oberösterreich*).

Though not as well known as some other provinces in Austria, the skiing around Obertraun is excellent, even boasting Austria's longest ski run – a daunting eleven kilometres. Nearby Dachstein has over forty lifts and a huge choice of piste for both skiers and snowboarders, and best of all is the fact that this little-known ski region has no queues or crowds.

The summer season is the busiest in Obertraun and the place becomes a haven for tourist activity. The Seerose Hotel is directly on the banks of Lake Hallstatt, which is popular for swimming, but it is also possible to enjoy hiking, caving, fishing, sailing and climbing. The Days really did chose a great place for capitalising on the tourist market, even if they did happen to stumble upon it accidentally.

For more information on Upper Austria, contact the Austrian National Tourist Board on +43 (0) 1/588 66-0 or visit http://www.austria-tourism.at. Alternatively, for more specific information on Obertraun, see http://www.tis-cover.at/obertraun

Culture

Austrians love their alcohol, and its consumption would probably rank as one of the most popular national pastimes. Whether your tipple is schnapps, wine or the local beer, you will find it available and in plentiful supply from as early as 9.30 a.m. This early-morning drinking (*Frühschoppen*) is very popular at weekends and is often accompanied by rowdy singing, accordions and yodelling.

If you fancy something a little more sedate to kick-start your day, perhaps a visit to the local *konditorei* would be preferable? These wonderful coffee and cake shops sell the best of both – you cannot open a *konditorei* unless you are a qualified master baker or chef, so top quality is guaranteed.

Another facet of Austrian culture that is worth being aware of is a certain penchant for nudity (*Freikörperkultur*). Never to be accused of prudishness, many Austrians like nothing better than to pass their summer holidays on nudist beaches or in summer camps. Fear not, however; if bearing all is not really your cup of tea, it is easily avoided: signs with the letters 'FKK' usually indicate a nudist area or activity, and 'FKK Strand' means nudist beach.

Transport

Public transport is excellent throughout Austria and it is possible to reach even the most remote little village by using the regular bus service, which runs frequently and on time. The bus and rail network is integrated, making it easy to switch from bus to train and vice versa, and covers the whole area comprehensively.

On the other hand, Austria's roads can be somewhat congested, particularly during the holiday season. The country also plays an important role in the communications and overland trade routes between much of Europe by virtue of its central position, resulting in an increased burden on its roads. In fact, transit traffic has been felt to damage the local communities and environment to such an extent that the government is developing a new transport strategy that will incorporate environmentally compatible forms of transport as well as state-of-the-art vehicle technology such as low-noise heavy goods vehicles. If you don't want to risk getting stuck on one of these Alpine roads en route to a neighbouring country, there are plenty of international airports at hand: Salzburg, Linz and Klagenfurt, for example. Try Ryanair for cheap flights from London Gatwick to all three, visit http://www.ryanair.com. Flybe (http://www.flybe.com) also offer good prices to Salzburg from Southampton and Birmingham. Alternatively Avro (http://www.avro.co.uk) often have deals to Salzburg.

Jobs

The current unemployment figure in Upper Austria is around 4 per cent, well below the 6.8 per cent recorded for Austria as a whole. Labour demand is primarily for skilled persons with specialist knowledge to work in the business, health and social service sectors. Seasonal tourism is also a big employer. There are very few part-time jobs available in Austria, and Upper Austria, making it problematic for single parents (particularly women with little mobility) to find work.

Konzession (Licence to Trade)

Setting up a business in Austria is more complicated than in the UK. In order to trade on your own you will need to apply to the Austrian authorities for a *Konzession*, and in order to obtain your *Konzession* you will need to have trained, qualified and gained work experience in your chosen profession. This means that rogue traders and cowboy builders simply do not exist in Austria . . . it also means that you will have to check that your qualifications are recognised and, if not, you may need to be prepared to retrain.

This was a problem for the Days when they arrived at their hotel. Although the Seerose was equipped with a restaurant and kitchen, neither Darron nor Lesley qualified for the *Konzession* necessary to run it for evening meals, despite both having spent years in the catering business. Darron has ambitions to retrain and get his *Konzession*, but in the meantime the restaurant will be sublet to a fully qualified Austrian chef.

Recruitment

The system for finding work in Austria is very similar to that of most EU member states. For a comprehensive guide to living and working in Austria you can visit the Jobcentre Plus website (http://www.jobcentreplus.gov.uk) following these links 'Looking for a job'> 'Working or training in Europe' > 'Austria'. Jobcentre Plus is part of a network of Public Employment Services that belong to the EURES system (European Employment Services). EURES is a partnership of the European Economic Area (EEA) that exchanges information on vacancies and living and working conditions within the union. Throughout the EEA there are around 500 specially trained EURES advisors on hand to help you with queries; those in the UK can be contacted through your local Jobcentre Plus office. The website (http://www.europa.eu.int) contains listings with job vacancies from all over Austria. Both EURES and Jobcentre Plus can also offer you help and advice on CVs, applications and vacancy listings. For more information you can call Jobseeker Direct on +44 (0) 845 606 0234.

The Austrian equivalent of Jobcentre Plus is *Arbeitsmarktservice-Geschäftsstelle* and any EEA member may use their services. Your nearest branch can be located through the telephone directory or through contacting the Head Office of the Austrian Employment Service.

> Bundesgeschäftsstelle
> Arbeitsmarktservice Österreich
> Dr Richard Bauer
> Treustrasse 35–43
> A-1200 Wien
> Tel: + 43 1 33 1780
> Website: http://www.ams.or.at

A list of private recruitment agencies can also be provided by this organisation or found on their website. If you are look-ing for vacancies on the Internet, you will need to look under *Jobsuche*.

In Austria the press is a very important source for job seekers. National and regional newspapers carry listings, particularly on Saturdays. Good publications to try are the *Kurier*, *Standard*, *Kleine Zeitung* and *Presse*. Another good resource for job hunting is the *Samsomat* – a self-service computer that holds information on local job opportunities. *Samsomat* can be found in any job centre in Austria; users simply print out the information they require.

House Prices
Property prices all over Austria have dropped in recent years primarily due to overbuild in the cities, a falling population and, of course, the recession that settled over all of Europe.

Being one of Austria's most famous and picturesque cities, Salzburg retains a good property market where you can expect to pay anything from €120,000 to €220,000 (£83,000 to £152,000) for an apartment or from €300,000 (£210,000) for a house. Out in the country is another story, however, and property can be bought fairly cheaply. In Obertraun you could probably pick up a nice apartment for €95,000 (£66,000) and a large house for around €240,000 (£166,000).

The house-buying process is very straightforward in Austria – once the offer document has been signed by both parties, the deal is done. There is no gazumping and you know exactly how much you will be paying for the property. Land Registry is a computerised system so your estate agent will be able to do an instant land search that will inform you who owns the land and property as well as uncovering issues such as outstanding mortgages and rights of way. Of course, the use of a lawyer is still recommended.

Tax
People living in Austria are subject to the following taxes:

1 Income Tax based on taxable earnings in one calendar year. Tax from employment income is deducted at the source along with social security contributions. These deductions are an advance payment on the year's tax, which is calculated and adjusted accordingly on the basis of your annual tax return.

   Individuals living in Austria for most of the year have unlimited tax liability on all income from foreign and domestic sources. Income from the following is taxable:

   Agriculture and forestry
   Self-employment
   Trade and commerce
   Employment
   Investment income
   Rental and leasing

   European Union members have signed Double Taxation Treaties, meaning that you will only be taxed once on income from any of these countries.
   Income tax is charged at a flat rate, meaning everyone pays the same amount; a person's marital/familial status is taken into account by way of tax relief. Tax deductions are also granted for special and extraordinary expenses such as home-care costs.

Tax brackets at the time of writing are as follows:

Income up to €3640: 0 per cent tax payable

Income between €3640–€7270: 21 per cent tax payable

Income between €7271–€21,800: 31 per cent tax payable

Income between €21,801–€50,870: 41 per cent tax payable

Income up to and over €50,871: 50 per cent tax payable

2   Inheritance and Gift Tax

3   Church Tax (this totals around 1.25 per cent of gross income and is paid to the religious community of which one is a member)

4   Property Acquisition Tax

5   Vehicle Tax (paid according to engine size)

6   Turnover Tax (an indirect tax on goods or services paid by the end user). The current rate is 10–20 per cent.

7   Corporation Tax

For more information contact:

Inland Revenue International Division (Double Taxation)

Victory House

30–34 Kingsway

London

WC2B 6ES

Tel: +44 (0) 20 7438 6622

The Inland Revenue website contains information on taxation and online versions of each of its forms: http://www.inlandrevenue.gov.uk.

In Austria you can contact:

Bundesministerium für Finanzen
Himmelpfortgasse 8
A-1014 Vienna
Tel: +43 (1) 51433
Website: http://www.bmf.gv.at

Residency

Nationals of European Union member states may live in Austria without a residence permit for up to three months providing they hold a valid identity document or national passport. Individuals from EU countries are exempt from visa requirements and can settle where they wish, but they must have adequate health insurance, sufficient funds and evidence that they are likely to find employment.

In Austria the registration of your address is compulsory and must be done within three days of taking up residence. Registration is done through the Registration Office (*Meldeamt*) at the Federal Police offices (*Bundespolizei-direktion*). You must take with you:

- A completed residence registration form (*Meldezettel*)

- Your passport and/or birth certificate

- Any previous residence registration forms

If you are going to change your address or leave Austria, you must let the authorities know within three days.

In order to apply for your residence permit (*EWR Lichtbildausweis*) you will need to take a completed application form to the local police station (*Polizei* or *Gendarmerie-Wachzimmer*). Applications and further information can be obtained from:

> Fremdenpolizeiliches Büro
> Wasagasse 22
> A-1090 Vienna
> Tel: + 43 (1) 313 440

Education

A free co-educational school system operates in Austria and is available to every child. Children resident in Austria are legally obliged to attend nine years of schooling, beginning at the age of six. Parents with children below the age of six can choose to send them to nursery, kindergarten or other pre-school institutions. These can be located by applying to the *Sozialreferat* at your local council offices (*Gemeindeamt*), or through offices for youth and family affairs (*Ämter für Jugend und Familie*).

The first four years of compulsory education are spent in primary school (*Volksschule*), after which children can attend secondary school (*Hauptschule*). The ninth and final year of compulsory schooling can be completed at other institutions such as polytechnic or vocational colleges. Most upper schools culminate in the school-leaving examination, or *Matura*, which entitles holders to attend academies, colleges and universities.

In order to register your child at school, you should make an appointment with the headmaster or headmistress. The child will need to attend the meeting and you will also need to take:

- A residence registration form (*Meldezettel*)
- Proof of citizenship or a valid passport
- A document indicating religious adherence
- Their birth certificate
- Their vaccination certificate

Private schooling is also widely available in Austria, though it is often Catholic and usually fees are applicable.

Health

There is a comprehensive and efficient public health service in Austria, though it only extends to the working population – if you wish to retire out there, you will need to seek separate advice or possibly even take out private health insurance. Everyone in paid employment – and their families – must join the government sickness insurance fund, which is partly funded by the employer and partly by the employee. Contributions to the scheme are usually deducted directly from your wages and will pay for doctor's visits, medicines and hospitalisation.

The required voucher – or *Krankenschein* – can be obtained from your employer and must be taken with you when you go to seek medical treatment. You can chose to see any doctor, and if you don't get along, the next time you need to visit you can simply chose someone else. For any queries regarding local doctors or other health issues contact your local area health office – *Gebietskrankenkasse* (GKK).

Hospitals are well equipped and have no waiting lists. If your doctor or specialist decides you require either hospital treatment or surgery, you will probably be booked in within a matter of days. As an Austrian resident you can also expect a free, full health check every two years.

Your medical records are your own and will be kept by you at home, so you must take your file along to any doctor you see.

Much of the information on these pages has come from EURES – the European Job Mobility Portal. For more information on any aspect of living and working abroad visit their website at http://www.europa.eu.int/eures/home. There is also a freephone helpline number: 00800 4080 4080.

A lot of information was also provided by Jobcentre Plus, who are part of the EURES network. For more information visit http://www.jobcentreplus.gov.uk or call Jobseekers Direct on +44 (0) 845 606 0234.

Additional information was supplied by David Potter.

You can also try the Austrian Embassy:

Austrian Embassy
18 Belgrave Mews West
London SW1X 8HU
Tel: +44 (0) 20 7235 3731
Fax: +44 (0) 20 7344 0292
Email: embassy@austria.org.uk
Website: http://www.austria.org.uk

CHAPTER 4

From Banstead to Brittany

Kevin Snuggs, partner Carol Hill and their girls Holly and Rosy were one of the first families featured on *No Going Back*. Three years on and their new life in Brittany is going well; all are happy, the carp-fishing business is established and they have a new addition to the family.

Kevin Snuggs, as I am sure anyone who watched either of their programmes will agree, is one of life's inspirers. When we were introduced to him, he owned a building company in Banstead and was regularly putting in six or seven days' work a week, but it was clear from the outset that he was destined for bigger and better things. Kevin shared his life, and home, with his partner Carol Hill and their two daughters Holly (ten) and Rosy (six); Carol also worked part-time. The family were settled and happy, but Kevin was to turn their existence upside down by announcing a new dream: he wanted to run a carp-fishing business.

'I had travelled for a long time when I was younger,' Kevin tells me. 'All over the place, Central and South America, New Zealand, Canada ... When I returned to England I found it really hard to settle. I did, of course – you have to – but I always knew that I wanted to do something a bit different.'

A keen angler, Kevin had made some enquiries and seen that there was a gap in the leisure fishing industry – it was a gap he felt sure he could fill. Embarking on some serious research into his project, it immediately became apparent that the property and land prices in England would be prohibitive, so Kevin extended his research across the Channel. It was on his second trip to France that he came across Clearwater Lakes and knew he'd stumbled upon something special. Now he just had to convince Carol.

'A fortnight after he'd seen it, Kevin took me out to have a look,' she explains. 'As soon as we came around the corner and got out of the car I have to say my jaw dropped. We were looking out over the lakes themselves and I just fell in love then and there. I turned to Kevin and just said, "I want to live here."

'At this point I hadn't even seen the house. The rest of the grounds, and the property itself, were overgrown, filthy and full of rubbish: it looked pretty terrible. Kevin is such an inspirational person, though – we were walking around the place and he was telling me about all these plans, and what we could do to improve it. To be honest, though, I didn't need much convincing. I found it surprisingly easy to see through it all and imagine us living there.'

With Carol very much on side, the couple's next job was to convince the children. They took lots of video footage and returned to show the girls. The family talked and went through everything until Holly and Rosy were as excited as Kevin and Carol. It wasn't long before the whole family was completely convinced that they should make the move to France. Reassured by the girls' enthusiasm, Kevin and Carol put in an offer on the French property which was duly accepted, and from there onwards there really was no going back. For the grand sum of £150,000 (€224,127), the family had secured themselves a twenty-eight-acre farm complete with dense woodland, two lakes (one ten-acre and one three-acre), a cottage, a disused water mill and several out-buildings. In contrast with what they could have bought in Devon for the same sum, the value for money was astounding. The property – soon to be christened Clearwater Lakes – was in the tiny, remote village of St Tugdual in the heart of rural Brittany. It was an idyllic location for a fishery.

In December 2000, Kevin packed up his car and set off on his one-way journey to Clearwater Lakes. As a qualified and experienced builder, he planned to do all the work on the property himself and his first job was to make the most prom-ising building – the cottage – habitable before Carol and the girls joined him. There was a lot to do. The farm had not been occupied for fifteen years so even the best building needed substantial work. Unfazed, Kevin installed flushing toilets, hot water, a shower, a new kitchen, and patched the leaking roof. By 2 January 2001 the family were reunited again, under the repaired roof of the Clearwater Lakes cottage.

They had a new home.

Prior to leaving the UK, Kevin and Carol had done a con-siderable amount of homework. They had spent time and money getting advice on setting up the fishing business and settling into French life. With this preparation under their belts, the couple felt sure that they would be able to open in time for the first fishing season in March of that same year.

Of course, it will come as no surprise to regular viewers of *No Going Back* that they were sadly mistaken. Despite their thorough research, Kevin and Carol stumbled at the first hurdle and quickly became stuck in the quicksand of the legendary French bureaucratic red tape. It seemed that obtaining the necessary fishing licences was not going to be as simple as they had anticipated.

'The bureaucracy is unbelievable,' exclaims Kevin. 'Even the French admit it really is something else. The worst thing is that no one seems to know what to do, not even the *notaires* (French lawyers). You can speak to two people working in the same department and they will tell you two entirely different things.

'It didn't take us long to realise that, even with the best will in the world, there was no way we were going to be open for the first season. It is strange because to this day I don't really understand what the problem was, though I have been told it was something to do with the classification of the lakes. It seems crazy, though, because I wasn't asking them for anything. I didn't want any money or help, I just wanted to set up my own business on my own land. We had paid someone in England to look into all this for us, but as soon as we actually got out here it was a different story. The goalposts kept moving. It ended up taking us nine months to get all the right paperwork needed to get the business started.'

Despite their frustration, the family realised there was little point in kicking up a fuss – there was plenty to do at

Clearwater Lakes, fishing licence or no fishing licence. First and foremost, the girls had to be settled into their new life and the local school. Their lifestyles had changed dramatically and Kevin and Carol were anxious about how well they would adjust. After just a couple of weeks, however, it seemed that they needn't have worried; the girls were taking to their new French lives very quickly. Both loved their new school, were enraptured by their new home and were rapidly picking up the language. Weekends could be spent roaming through the woods and playing within the twenty-eight acres that was now their back garden. Carol was also delighted with her new surroundings. 'It is strange but it felt like home immediately,' she muses. 'I thought it would take much longer and was amazed at how quickly we all got used to it and grew to love it. I guess for me home is wherever we are all together, so us all being here and all being happy just made it the perfect place.'

With the family settled and content, the next priority was to get enough work done on the lakes and facilities to allow the business to open. As Kevin saw it, Clearwater Lakes was a ten-year project. He had grand plans for converting all the outbuildings into facilities for the anglers, and his pet project was to be the watermill that he would eventually convert into the family home. As he anticipated doing all the work himself, without the help of a building team, he had had to factor in realistic timescales. Nor was there a huge amount of capital to cover all the work. There was enough to get started and from there onwards profits from the business would be ploughed straight back in as and when Kevin could get on with the work. However, in order to open the business there was some essential work that had to be done in the first year. This included ensuring that the lakes were clean and safe enough to hold the carp, installing a usable track right around each lake so the anglers could easily access all the swims and camp comfortably, and, finally, one of the out-buildings had to be converted into a shower and toilet block for the anglers.

One of the first jobs that Kevin undertook was to drain one of the two large lakes on the property, ensuring that there were no unwelcome predators to threaten his prize carp when they were stocked. It was an almighty task, and despite his propensity to work unaided, Kevin had to enlist the help, and expertise, of two locals. Nothing too ferocious was uncovered at the bottom of the lakes, but the discovery of a giant catfish weighing in at 101 pounds caused some waves. The ugly monster was hurriedly dispatched to a local fishery.

Two clean, predator-free lakes later, and the family's next task was clearing some of the tangle of brambles and undergrowth that was encroaching upon the lakes. A clear path was needed for the anglers and to facilitate Kevin's rounds. Carol and the girls helped with the hard labour and the family made good headway. The shower block was a job to be taken on by Kevin alone. He worked away heroically but because the business couldn't open as planned and it seemed as if it would not be pulling in any money for the first year – or at least until the fishing licences were sorted out – it was only a matter of months before the family's savings began to dwindle.

'In that first year I had also planned to build a clubhouse for the anglers,' admits Kevin. 'Not earning anything put that on hold. I had also hoped to do some more work on our own house as it was all a bit temporary . . . that went out of the window too. It was pretty tough financially, and emotionally. There were times when we thought we would never get the licences and that we wouldn't be able to open at all. I had to sell my beloved MG to finish doing the work I had started. It was worth the sacrifice, though – as Carol pointed out I only ever drove it twice a year – and the extra money meant that I was able to finish everything that was essential for the business in that first year. The rest would just have to wait until Clearwater Lakes had earned us some money.'

Another part of the family's dream of moving to France was to become self-sufficient. With the fishing business on hold, this aspect could be concentrated on as it was also hoped it would save them some substantial money. Kevin wasted no time building a chicken coop, which he filled with chicks, and it wasn't long before goats and sheep also joined the menagerie at Clearwater Lakes. Once the chicks had grown they did their owners proud, producing plenty of eggs, which were collected by Holly and Rosy each day. The other livestock proved a little more problematical, however. The sheep quickly became seen as family pets, rather than food as was their intended purpose. Having had to agree that the original 'pets' could remain as breeding animals, Kevin warned Holly and Rosy not to get so attached to any offspring produced, as they would not be allowed the lucky escape bestowed on their parents. A large vegetable patch was inaugurated too, replete with carrots, parsnips, broccoli, courgettes, strawberries and lettuces. Sadly, though, it seems that for all of Kevin's many talents, the gift of green fingers had eluded him. After back-breaking hours from both him and Carol, the results were paltry. They remained undeterred, however.

Throughout the financial tension and French bureaucratic nightmare, the whole family remained very happy and convinced that their decision had been the right one; that Clearwater Lakes was their rightful home. Their faith paid off when in September 2001, nine months after their initial application, Kevin and Carol were presented with a licence to get the business running with immediate effect. The St Tugdual *Mairie* had finally come through for them.

As ever, Kevin reacted quickly. He had set aside a budget of £40,000 (€60,000)to purchase his batch of top-quality carp and he was delighted when they were unloaded. They were beautiful specimens and none of them had ever been fished. Seeing them released, one by one, into the lake was very satisfying. At least now they knew for sure that they would be able to open – and earn an income – during the next season. Their future in Brittany was assured . . . or at least it would be if they could get the bookings they needed.

It was not too long before the start of their first fishing season that Carol became pregnant. With the business about to get underway as well, the news had come at an already exciting time and all of the family were delighted.

'It was a bit of a shock,' admits Carol, 'but a very welcome one. We were about to open Clearwater Lakes for business and even though there was still a lot to do on the place, it seemed right to put down more roots here. I had no qualms at all about bringing a child up in France. Holly and Rosy had fitted in straight away and just absolutely loved life, and even school! Within six months they were just so, so French. If a stranger watched them playing with their French friends he would never guess that they were actually English. They are both sociable, bright children, but I really do think that the key to their success was their ages when we moved. When we first arrived they both went straight into primary school. Of course it was daunting for them, but it was also a fun atmosphere. They were able to learn the language while painting, playing games, working out puzzles and making friends. I think secondary school is entirely different because at that stage you have to pick up a language through difficult geography and science lessons; there is also far more social pressure. Had Holly been at secondary school before we moved we really would have thought twice about coming here. I don't think she would have thrived nearly as well as she has. Obviously the new arrival would be starting from scratch so he or she would be well integrated almost immediately.'

The first season was looking promising. The website had had a lot of hits and there were a few bookings in Carol's database. Kevin had reckoned that in order to cover the setting-up costs and give himself some capital to do further renovations at Clearwater Lakes, he needed to pull in about one hundred anglers over the nine-month season – eight per week at peak times.

'We were doing okay in terms of bookings,' says Kevin. 'But when the *No Going Back* programme showed in the UK the phone just went mad. We had literally thousands of emails, I couldn't believe it. Of course most of them were well-wishers or people asking advice about doing something similar, but there were plenty of bookings too. We ended up having over one hundred and fifty anglers staying with us.'

'Kevin was really in his element,' Carol comments proudly. 'He did the rounds every day, chatting to the anglers and delivering them timely bacon butties. We had great feedback from people, and a lot of repeat bookings. It was brilliant to finally be up and running and making a success of it, even if it was a year later than planned!' The season ended in November, but far from being able to put their feet up, there was still plenty to do around Clearwater Lakes now that more capital had come in.

In December 2002 Sydney Fay was born at the nearby hospital and, after a traumatic birth, was brought home to join her overjoyed family.

'The girls just adore having a baby sister,' enthuses Carol. 'And having her here in France has meant that Kevin can spend a lot of time with her too, which just wouldn't have been possible in the UK, so it is brilliant for all of us. Being pregnant in France was very different to my other experiences but I received excellent care from the local midwife. Between the consultant's English, and Kevin's and my French, we were able to communicate pretty well. There was one slight problem, though – the French are absolutely mad on testing for toxoplasmosis; I guess it is because we are in such a rural area. They were very strict with me throughout the pregnancy; I couldn't go near the sheep while they were lambing or eat red meat. Anyway, after one particular visit, something got lost in translation and I came home convinced I had toxoplasmosis. I got myself into a complete state, trying to look it up on the Internet and figure out just how much damage it could do. The whole misunderstanding was sorted out within a matter of minutes on my next visit, though. Both me and the baby were fine!'

Clearwater Lakes had an excellent second season too and the family continued to go from strength to strength during their third year in Brittany. Of course there were hard times, but never for one minute have any of them thought about returning; in fact, Holly has threatened to lock herself in her room if anyone so much as suggests a return to the UK.

'Don't get me wrong, though,' warns Kevin. 'It is not a bed of roses. After seeing the programme lots of people thought Carol and I never argued – of course it isn't as sugar-coated as that. For a lot of people "the dream" is to sit outside all day sipping wine and nibbling cheese – we haven't had a single day like that. There is so much to do maintaining the lakes, carrying on the renovation of the clubhouse, setting up a shop, or building a barbecue area – it just doesn't stop really. When we moved out here I had a ten-year plan for the business; three years on and it is still a ten-year plan; I think in five years' time it will still be a ten-year plan. Some days I work harder here than I did in the UK, but I enjoy the work and it is my choice. I can see my family whenever I want to. To be honest, I can't ever foresee a day when there is nothing to do on the place, and if or when that day does come, it'll probably be the day I sell. I couldn't bear a life of wine-sipping and cheese-nibbling, I need a challenge.'

*

Kevin, Carol, Holly, Rosy and Sydney are now in their fourth year of life in Brittany and Clearwater Lakes is halfway through its third season. There is still plenty of work to do but all are very happy.

'The business is going so, so well,' smiles Carol. 'This year we have had quite a few Dutch anglers come and stay with us . . . we are becoming international! There are a lot of English people coming over here now to open carp-fishing lakes, and a lot of them are struggling. We aren't too worried about the competition, though; we are well established and have a lot of regular clients, most of whom we now consider friends.

'Kevin is still working really hard to get more facilities built. I am looking forward to the day that he can start work on our own house, though. At the moment everything is about the business. From March to November we eat, sleep and breathe the business, which is fair enough, but our living conditions haven't improved much since we first moved out here. Don't get me wrong, it's not as though we are living in squalor, but it would be nice to think that plans for our own house aren't in the too distant future now!'

The family have adopted the French lifestyle remarkably easily, getting to know neighbours and enjoying wonderful meals and the occasional glass of local cider. Holly and Rosy have a large circle of friends from school and the other activities they participate in, and both are doing very well academically. Kevin and Carol have found less time to meet people, however, because they spend so much time on the business.

'We do have some good friends,' says Kevin, 'but during

the season – and that is nine months of the year – I rarely leave Clearwater Lakes. When I do it is to go and get supplies or building materials, so it is very hard to make time for socialising.

'Language can still be a problem too. Because Carol and I spend so much time with the anglers, we don't practise our French as much as we'd like. There is the added difficulty here of the Breton language: it is as different to French as Welsh is to English and lots of people here speak it. Even those that don't often have heavy accents, so it can be hard.'

'Our French hasn't come along as much as we would have liked,' agrees Carol. 'Holly and Rosy have been brilliant at helping us as they are virtually fluent now. It is very strange to rely on your daughters like that, though – it drives me mad, to be honest. I'm the mum, I should be looking after them, but sometimes it feels like the other way round.

'We don't have as many friends as we had in England but friendships take time and we haven't been here that long. One thing I do miss is time just with Kevin. In England we were surrounded by friends and family who could be called on to babysit, but here it is far more difficult. It is strange that I am very rarely "Carol" any more – I spend almost all my time as "Mum". Not that I mind at all . . . the amount of time we get to spend as a family really does compensate and that was part of the original reason for coming here after all.'

One thing that the family hadn't prepared themselves for was the number of British people they would find in Brittany.

Their chosen location, St Tugdual, is small and rural, so the last thing they expected was an invasion from the UK.

'When we first moved in we thought we were the only English people around,' says Kevin. 'We were amazed to find a couple already installed here. Since then it has just gone mad, there are so many English swarming in and they all seem to be running *gîte* complexes too. We have a few English friends but most are French.

'As a result of the influx, property prices have rocketed, You just can't get that barn in need of renovation with lots of land for £10,000 any more – it is more likely to cost you £70,000. We get emails all the time from people wanting to get something like Clearwater Lakes for £150,000, which is what we paid, which just isn't going to happen. These days you would need three times that.'

Of course this doesn't pose any problems for Kevin, Carol, Holly, Rosy and Sydney, who have absolutely no intention of going anywhere. Through luck or judgement they made their move at the right time and were able to get a business established and set to thrive with just a small outlay.

'We are never going to make a fortune here,' Kevin levels. 'But the move was never about that. It was about our lifestyles and I can honestly say that none of us have ever been happier.'

'We're about to receive another new addition to the family too,' beams Carol. 'The new baby is due on 20 August, which is the date we had originally set as my and Kevin's wedding; needless to say, that that has been postponed! It will be wonderful to have another child but we have decided that that will be it then.

Clearwater Lakes is open from March to November and a week's fishing costs from £240. On-site facilities (toilets, showers and sinks) are available and a clubhouse will be opening shortly. For more information on fishing, view the excellent website: http://www.clearwaterlakes.com.

Top Tips

Kevin and Carol offer some advice:

- Don't fall in love with a dream. It is not about drinking wine and nibbling cheese, there is some serious work involved. On paper it looks fantastic – great lifestyle, more family time – but think about it seriously. Competition is very high now in this region and getting established might be more difficult than you had ever imagined – you probably won't have a Channel 4 programme behind you!

- You need to consider lots of things. Are you going to do the renovation yourself? If you are, it could take years; if you are not, it will be expensive. Prices of tradesmen and builders here are the same as in Britain; some materials are cheaper, some are more expensive. A lot of people assume that because it is France it will be cheaper . . . it's not. This also applies to things like food. We spend the same on our weekly grocery bill now as we did in England; the fruit and vegetables are of a higher quality here, no doubt, but they cost the same. Diesel is cheaper here but you have to drive much further to get anywhere because we are so rural. It's all relative.

- Be careful when you buy a property – there are lots of things you won't know about and your agent might not either. We have some English friends who bought a lovely farmhouse from an English agent. What they didn't know, and what they couldn't have known until they moved in, is that the farmer who lives up the hill from them has access rights to the track that runs right in front of their house. As a result, they are often woken at dawn by his tractor or muckspreader rumbling past. When they fell out with the farmer he parked his tractor next to their front door – there was nothing they could do because he was legally allowed to be there.

- Don't buy through an English agent as they will add their commission on top of the house price. Always use a French *notaire*.

- Living the village life means lots of rumours. We were out last week picking up building supplies from a town about a forty-minute drive away when we ran into another English couple living in the region. We got talking because they recognised us from the television programme, and it turns out that they had heard we are selling. A lot of people hear that about us actually. The other big rumour is that we have won the lottery. We've actually had people come and knock on the door to ask us these things!

- Research. You've got to spend both time and money looking into things before you come out. You will still come across a hundred things you didn't know, but at least you are familiar with some of it. We've had thousands of emails from people asking us how to do it; everything from how to register your kids in school to how to buy a second-hand tractor. We haven't got time to answer all of these – I'm afraid we're not a consultancy. You have to find out for yourself, otherwise how will you ever learn? We don't know everything yet but we are getting there – it has had Carol in tears many times before now because there is so much red tape, but, to be frank, you've just got to get on with it. It's not like in England, where you fill everything in and then that's it until your circumstances change – here you have to do it annually. Every year it is more forms, forms, forms. Try to photocopy everything and keep it: it might make things easier next year.

Practical Directory – Brittany

Region

Situated in France's north-west corner, Brittany is culturally and geographically distinct from the rest of France. Its coastline is often compared to Cornwall on account of its famed rugged beauty, the secluded sandy beaches and traditional fishing villages found here that draw visitors from far and wide. If you are seeking that warm, dry Mediterranean climate do not head to Brittany as it experiences weather patterns similar to those experienced in Blighty. However, the diverse scenery – from giant prehistoric megaliths and wooded river valleys to the rolling moorlands of Finistère – more than compensates.

Another of Brittany's big plus points from the British perspective is its incredible accessibility: in fact, to live in the area and commute to work in the UK is not unheard of. It is a land that appeals to holidaymakers and homemakers of all ages, boasting lovely open countryside, traffic-free roads, small towns and cosmopolitan resorts. For further information visit http://www.franceway.com, http://www.westernfrance-tourist board.com or http://www.brittanytourism.com.

Culture

Brittany is famous for the Celtic culture that still thrives there and is manifest in the local language, festivals, music and dance. Food too is an important aspect of Brittany's heritage with many local specialities – such as moules marinières and crêpes – now thought of as quintessentially French. Most socialising here is done over lengthy and mouth-watering meals, but do look out for the cider (Lambig), which can be lethal.

A visit to one of Brittany's numerous religious festivals or *pardons* is highly recommended. Far from dour, these *fest noz'* are lively events accompanied by a lot of music, dancing and drinking.

Some wonderful examples of the mysterious menhir that have baffled archaeologists and historians alike for centuries still stand tall and proud in southern Brittany. Thought to have been constructed around 5,000 BC, there are some 3,000 alignments in the area which is now known to be one of the most important centres of megalithic culture in western Europe. The largest known menhir in the world stood in

Locmariaquer. Although it has long since given way to the strong Breton winds and shattered into four parts, it once stood twenty metres high and weighed a crippling 350 tonnes.

Transport

Brittany is one of the easiest parts of Europe to access from England. There are regular and economical ferry crossings from Weymouth, Poole, Newhaven, Dover, Portsmouth and Folkestone to (in order of proximity to Kevin and the family) St Malo, Cherbourg, Le Havre, Dieppe and Calais. These services are run by Brittany Ferries (http://www.brittanyferries.co.uk), P&O Ferries (http://www.poferries.com) and Condor Ferries (http://www.condorferries.co.uk) – please view the individual websites for precise routes, times and prices. Roscoff is the closest port to Clearwater Lakes.

The Channel crossing can also be made via Eurostar (http://www.eurotunnel.co.uk). Train journeys take as little as thirty-five minutes and cost from £103 return for a car. From arrival in Calais, the drive time down to Clearwater Lakes will be around six to seven hours.

Ryanair (http://www.ryanair.com) operates flights from London Stansted to Brest and Dinard on Brittany's beautiful coastline.

Jobs

Brittany's biggest industry is food production, accounting for some 30 per cent of industrial employment. It is the most important region in France in terms of fishing, pig rearing, poultry farming and vegetable production.

Other boom industries include electronics and telecommunications. This north-west corner of France is also the second most important tourist region in France; this combined with its accessibility makes it a prime place to set up a rental or holiday-let business. Kevin saw a gap in the tourist market in Brittany and went for it, with great success.

Labour vacancies in the region at the time of writing include cooks (primarily for pizzas and crêpes), waiters and waitresses (on a seasonal basis), food processing industry workers and skilled construction workers – but wages are extremely low.

Recruitment
See Chapter 2

House Prices
The property market in Brittany is very buoyant and making an investment here often proves astute. Properties are cheap in comparison with much of France and the UK – although you will pay a premium for being close to the beach – and letting is easy on account of the accessibility. On top of this Brittany is a highly marketable area so selling up will rarely be a problem. Having said this, Kevin warns that the buy-to-let market is being flooded in the region.

'There are a lot of *gîte* complexes and many Brits hope to make money. It is, in my opinion, completely unsustainable because, although the number of people coming to Brittany on holiday is increasing, more and more are staying with friends now. I would seriously advise thinking twice about buying in Brittany to let to tourists: you might find that you only make pocket money.'

Properties are available in all manner of shapes, sizes and price brackets in Brittany. Traditional Breton style is characterised by long, low granite houses, stone cottages with slate roofs or large, double-fronted farmhouses. In addition, there are still renovation properties to be found, as well as newer properties, which are always built in the traditional Breton style. Property prices are reasonable, although these days you will have to pay far more than Kevin and Carol did for a property: for example, a small holiday home can be yours from around £70,000 (€104,600), whereas larger stone houses with three bedrooms and a garden can be found from £100,000 (€149,440). Character properties start at around £200,000 (€299,000).

Tax
See Chapter 2

Residency
See Chapter 2

Education
See Chapter 2

Health
See Chapter 2

Useful Contacts
Information in this chapter relating to jobs has come from EURES – the European Job Mobility Portal. For

more information on any aspect of living and working abroad visit their website at http://www.europa.eu.int. There is also a freephone helpline number: 00800 4080 4080.

CHAPTER 5

From Clevedon to Queensland

When Pete Piscina had to leave his beloved job with the Fire Service his wife Shirley knew it would be difficult for him to take a serious interest in any other profession, so she encouraged him to follow his dream.

'Pete lived for being a fireman,' explains Shirley. 'He was devastated when an injury to his arm while on the job meant that he had to be pensioned out. It really made him question what life was all about.'

This enormous upheaval in his professional life forced Pete to think about what direction his life should take in order to help him find happiness and fulfilment. Looking back over his past experiences, one of the happiest chapters he could recall was living and working in Australia when he was twenty.

'I guess that is where the idea came from,' admits Shirley,

'and after a few more discussions, Pete invested some money in a landscape garden business over there and we decided to apply for visas.'

They contacted the Australian High Commission and received mountains of application forms, which were duly filled in. Only after twelve months of waiting and expectation did the family find out that they did not qualify for the visa.

With hopes for a new life in Australia dashed, the Piscinas began to look around for something else to invest the money from Pete's pension in. At this time they were living in Clevedon with their three children Giorgia, Ella and newly born Gianni. Their opportunity arose close to home; a shop nearby was coming up for sale. The couple saw their chance and bought the premises outright as an investment. 'My sister was going to manage the shop and Pete was going to work in it; there was also a large empty space upstairs which Pete set about converting into an apartment. It was a bit of a project for him.'

The shop was established as a fashion accessories boutique, selling everything from jewellery and gifts to hairpieces, and the business did very well.

Things rolled on this way for about three years, by which time Pete had finished the apartment conversion. It was 2001 and business was better than they had ever hoped. The next natural step would be to buy another shop and become a chain; however, neither of them wanted to buy something in the vicinity, or, for that matter, in the UK.

On holiday in Mexico later that year, the family spent a day fishing on an idyllic beach. The tranquillity inspired

Pete to comment that it would be his dream to run a deep-sea fishing business in Australia. It dawned on Shirley that, now that they owned and ran their own business, they might be in a better position to apply for the Australian visa once more. It was decided then and there that, upon their return, they would make some enquiries and, that if they were going to pursue the visa, they would use an agent.

'We really couldn't believe it when we found out that to get a business visa for entry to Australia you have to have owned a business for three years and have turned over £215,000 in at least two of those years,' exclaims Shirley. 'There were other criteria too and we had fulfilled them without trying, or even realising.'

The Piscinas decided that, even with this crucial factor on their side, they would stick to their guns and use an agent to help them obtain their visa. With all the paperwork and legalities that were involved, the money seemed well spent and would hugely increase their chances of success. They were filling out forms by December, and by May 2002 the Piscinas had their visa: they were thrilled.

'Although the Australian idea was Pete's dream rather than mine, I was more than happy to make the move,' explains Shirley. 'As well as the shop, I was working full-time as a sales manager, I had four staff beneath me, a company car, phone, great salary . . . all the perks, but I had been working for the same company for eight years and I was bored – I'm that kind of person! I wanted to do something new.

'I also wanted to spend more time with my kids. We had

a nanny in Clevedon and it seemed so wrong to me that I was working and earning in order to pay for a nanny to look after my kids so that I could stay away from home more, work more and earn more money. It was a vicious circle and I wanted to get out. Even the promise of imminent promotion did nothing for me: it would just have meant even more hours at work.'

Naturally, the kids themselves were thrilled about the prospect of moving to the land of *Home and Away* and *Neighbours*, and this too buoyed up Shirley and Pete.

'Giorgia was seven, Ella was four and Gianni was three when we got the visa. It was a perfect time. None of the kids were too settled in Clevedon; they had playmates, of course, but they weren't being ripped away from any deep-rooted friendships. The idea of life in the sun and near a beach was appealing to all of us.'

The smoothness of the visa application meant that things in England had to be wrapped up fairly quickly. The family had a lot of capital tied up in the UK and wanted to sink all of it into their Australian adventure and the deep-sea fishing business. There was a shop, an apartment, the family's own home and a set of garages that they owned to be sold. All were put on the market, and with a little quick thinking from Shirley, the house and the garages were speedily, and profitably, sold.

This gave the family the funds they needed to move, and so, leaving the shop and apartment on the market, they made plans for the move itself. Of course, moving to Australia is logistically very different from moving somewhere within Europe and high moving costs needed to be calculated into the budget. The services of a professional removal company had to be called upon and, in due course, the Piscinas' belongings were ruthlessly sorted through, and either discarded or packed.

For their last few weeks in England, with their belongings having already begun their long journey and their home sold, the family lived in rented accommodation, and before long they too set off for Australia.

'Finally arriving there was fantastic,' says Shirley. 'It was hot, sunny, and it just felt like the start of an amazing holiday. We were all in really high spirits.' As their furniture was still some eight weeks away from joining them, the family booked into a motel on the beach. Prior to their departure from the UK, Pete had drawn up a business plan including a detailed budget. He had also located and recruited an experienced skipper, John Green. It was John who had all the necessary knowledge to get the fishing business off the ground and he was therefore the key to the Piscinas' success – Pete was relying on him 100 per cent. John was hired on a six-month contract that was agreed from England and paid a retainer until the Piscinas arrived. As John, the company's first and only employee, lived in Deception Bay in Queensland, the family decided to settle nearby, in Scarborough, around a half-hour drive from Brisbane. Though beyond reasonable reach of the Gold Coast – where many tourists went specifically to charter boats for deep-sea fishing – John assured them that their location would allow them to catch plenty of business from Brisbane itself.

Although she admits the decision was pretty arbitrary, Shirley was happy with Scarborough as it was beautiful, had a lovely beach and property prices in the area were still fairly reasonable despite the Australian property boom. After a week of rest and relaxation, during which the family sunbathed, barbecued and swam, it was decided that the time had come to get down to business.

The Piscinas had gained entry to Australia on a 457 Business Visa which meant they had stringent targets to meet in order to be allowed to remain in the country. Within four years of living in Australia, Pete's business would have to employ two native Australians, turn over in excess of £70,000 (A$171,740) per year and he would have to prove that he had invested around £45,000 (A$110,400) into the business, as well as having net assets of around £105,000 (A$257,628) in Australia.

(NB. The criteria for Australian visas change regularly. Please contact the Australian High Commission for details. The pressure was on for their deep-sea fishing charter business, Totally Offshore Fishing, to succeed, and within four years, otherwise the family could find themselves back in Clevedon.

The first task for Pete was to find a boat on which to carry his paying customers, so he and John set to work. The budget allowed for this crucial piece of equipment was around £100,000 (A$245,000), but all sensibly laid plans went out of the window when Pete fell in love with a top of the range model, Shakara. The luxurious custom-built forty-foot boat, which came complete with computerised navigation system, sophisticated fish-finding gear and a leather-clad interior, had a price tag that matched its impressive specification, a daunting £200,000 (A$490,000).

'I couldn't believe it,' admits Shirley. 'This meant that most of our money would be spent on the boat. I just didn't think he could be serious. I had plans to buy a house and get settled down comfortably, but all this went out the window when Pete fell for that damn boat!'

In spite of her misgivings, Shirley was persuaded to look at the boat as an investment and it was bought for the princely sum of £170,000 (A$419,640), though once fully kitted out and given a full service, the price weighed in once more at a hefty £180,000 (A$444,258).

Now it was Shirley's turn to leap into action. The novelty of living in a beachside motel had worn off and her main priorities for the family were a car and a home. The car, a four-wheel-drive Pajero, was purchased with relative ease and continues to serve the family to this day; however, now that buying a property outright was out of the question, finding a home was slightly more complex. The only option was to rent somewhere.

'I was told that I would never be able to find something to rent on the waterfront, it was just too in demand,' recalls Shirley. 'I was determined, though. Apart from the obvious appeal of living near water, we would be able to berth the boat ourselves and save on marina fees. We already had John's wages, the motel bill and other living expenses coming out of what was left of our account; I certainly didn't want any additional outgoings until we were earning.'

With grim determination, Shirley began daily visits to all the local estate agents to see what was on offer, and to remind them of what she wanted. Amazingly, before long, her persistence paid off. She secured the family a beautiful five-bedroom house with a swimming pool in a prime water-front position. And the price? At £650 (A$1594) per month it was an absolute steal!

With the family now installed in their luxurious rented home, and their magnificent boat moored at the end of their pontoon, Shirley was able to relax, enjoy the sunshine, concentrate on looking after Gianni and help settle Ella and Giorgia into their new school. Unfortunately, the bliss was short-lived.

'I wanted Pete and John to get the boat earning as soon as possible; after all the money we'd thrown at it, it really needed to start paying for itself. All I ever seemed to see was them sitting at the end of the pontoon talking and drinking tea. I realise there must have been a lot to talk about but there was no action at all and this wound me up no end. I don't sit down, ever, so to see money regularly going out of our account for repairs, not to mention John's retainer, infuriated me and I gradually lost patience. Did they think customers were just going to come knocking at the door? In hindsight, Pete was working extremely hard, but our skipper seemed to have no interest in promoting the business. We were suffering because we had been relying on his experience a little too much.

'After what felt like months of nagging, I decided to take the initiative myself.'

Shirley set to work doing what she knew best after years in marketing and sales. She had brochures, flyers and business cards printed and also designed a website for the business. John and Pete were clearly pleased with what Shirley had done and Pete helped to distribute a lot of the material. Once again Shirley sprang into action delivering her wares to all the local bars, hotels and restaurants.

'This was a real low point for me,' admits Shirley. 'There was constant tension between me and Pete that has never been there before, or since. For about six months we were just constantly sniping at each other. With hindsight it is easy to see what was going on. Pete is really practical and handy, but he's not a phone or computer person like I am. I was just doing a role that came naturally to me and was wondering why it didn't come naturally to Pete. This was all compounded by my anxieties about money – we still hadn't sold the shop or the apartment in England and I resented that boat and the fact that I wasn't relaxing, as planned. I didn't have anything for me either; plenty of money was going out of our account that, in my opinion, should have been going on our house.'

When she found out that there were buyers interested in both their remaining properties in England, Shirley was determined to tie up the money from the sales. She didn't want it to just drain away paying John's wage or for more equipment for the boat, so she began looking for a plot of land to buy on which they could build their dream home. Then, out of the blue, Pete announced that he had found it. A sign that had just gone up that morning advertised a large canalside plot just a short drive away.

Pete tore down there.

'We were so lucky. The land had been sold some weeks previously but the buyers were messing the seller around and hadn't completed on the sale. Just as they were backing out, we were pulling up and I literally said to the seller before even finding out the price 'We'll have it.' We signed then and there and laid down a hefty deposit.'

This was a real gamble for Shirley. The sale of their remaining properties in the UK would fund the purchase of the land, but no commitments had yet been made by their buyer. If he backed out and the sale didn't go through, the Piscinas stood to lose their plot, and their deposit.

Amazingly, everything came together as planned. With a plot for her house secured, and the remaining money from the sale of the UK property banked, Shirley was a lot happier and more relaxed.

'We had met some wonderful people out here, and in spite of everything, I couldn't help but enjoy myself,' she smiles. 'The sun was shining and for the first time in my working life I had the time to build friendships. We made more friends in our first year of living in Australia than in all those years living in Clevedon. Both Pete and I are far more active socially now. Living on a canal is like *Neighbours*: everybody knows everybody else and there is always some social activity or other – usually barbies!'

The kids too were very happy and had settled into the Australian way of life. The Catholic school Ella and Giorgia attended was just down the road and they had made lots of friends there. Giorgia was proving to be an exceptional student and a potential Olympic-standard gymnast. All three were enjoying living their lives outdoors and in the sun; Gianni was rarely out of the pool and a full-size trampoline in the front garden provided hours of fun for them and their friends. The marketing that Shirley had done for the business started to provide dividends too, as bookings and enquiries started coming in and Totally Offshore Fishing's first charter was scheduled.

The boat was a knockout, seriously impressing all their customers, John came into his own and found them plenty of fish to play with and, despite his nerves, Pete did a tremendous job as deckhand. The day was a complete success with the happy punters promising to make a repeat booking soon. More successful bookings followed and Pete proved to be in his element. Happy and relaxed, things were really coming together for the family.

And then disaster struck. The spring brought with it the worst storms seen in Queensland for many years. Pete had to cancel almost all his bookings, losing over £9000 (A$22,200) worth of business in the process. This was a huge blow both financially and psychologically. After all the months of waiting the business was finally starting to come together and now he had to turn away potential clients.

'We always knew we weren't going to make a huge income from Totally Offshore Fishing,' says Shirley, 'but all we really wanted was enough to fulfil our visa requirements and secure our future in Australia. The move wasn't about making money, it was about our lifestyles. It was hard not to worry when there was no money coming in, though.' With this thought perhaps in the back of her mind, but also due to her inimitable ambition and drive, Shirley accidentally ended up going into business herself.

'I was helping a friend run a stand at a fashion exhibition in July and I couldn't help but notice that there was no hair there,' she explains. 'I think the reason this really jumped out at me was because in our shop in Clevedon, hairpieces had always been a very profitable line. I asked my friend if, at her next exhibition, I could share her stand and sell hairpieces. She thought it was a great idea.'

The next exhibition was in February the following year, giving Shirley around six months to plan the whole thing. She needed to do market research, find good quality suppliers, work out the costs and check her plan was viable. All the indications were that the idea was a good one. The next step was to do some conceptualisation. Shirley needed a logo, a slogan and, most importantly, a name for the business. Shortly afterwards Totally Hair Direct ('because life's too short to wait for long hair') was born. It was an instant success at the exhibition and the hairpieces Shirley had imported sold like hot cakes. With this resounding triumph fresh in her mind, Shirley hired two marketing assistants and began repping around salons, selling the hairpieces wholesale. Within two months Totally Hair Direct had been a huge success, supplying sixty salons nationwide.

'The business has taken off really quickly,' Shirley beams. 'With hindsight I think it was pretty naive of me to think I would just be happy to relax. I'm not that kind of person. The fishing business would never have been enough for me either; we've initiated a few competitions and other ideas, but generally all the work involves – if you're not actually out on the boat – is dealing with queries and taking bookings. Totally Hair Direct really suits me. Its success is contributing to our visa application and because it is wholesale I don't have to be anywhere at any particular time. My life can revolve around the kids and I can fill the rest with work.'

Since the cameras left the Piscinas, their respective empires have gone from strength to strength. Totally Offshore Fishing has become known as one of the best charters in the area and its success has generated plenty of exposure for Pete with television appearances and a front-page picture on *Queensland Monthly* magazine. The boat is recognised as one of the best in the business and in competition usually produces at least one prize-winning angler. Pete himself has won the coveted Moreton Bay trophy. Arguably, though, their greatest claim is that during the Rugby World Cup the French national team chartered their boat for a day's fishing. Sadly, the adventure had to be called off when their coach caught wind of the plan and cancelled it on the grounds that they were unable to take seasickness tablets. As compensation Shirley and Pete received a signed Rugby shirt and ball. With such great publicity, the bookings are taking care of themselves, by his own admission Pete is unable to leave the room without the phone ringing and he is out on charters three or four times a week.

Totally Hair Direct is still doing very well too and Shirley has plans to launch the business in Europe. In November 2003 she exhibited at The Clothes Show at Birmingham NEC, and in addition to selling all her stock found interested distributors in Germany and France. Her hairpieces are being trialled in two further chains across Australia, and she is optimistic that at least one of the contracts will come through. If her success continues she will take on another member of staff and the couple should sail through the entry visa requirements. Shirley isn't counting her chickens, however.

'The worst thing about all our experiences here has without doubt been the uncertainty of whether we would be able to stay. We have worked really hard and this place is now our home. The kids are unbelievably happy here and so are Pete and I. Planning approval on the house we designed came through a couple of months ago. There was a lot of nipping and tucking, which is why it has taken so long, but it's not every day that you get to design and build your own house! We've just got to keep our fingers crossed that our businesses continue doing well and that we meet the visa criteria. We are willing to work our backsides off to get it . . . to have to go back now would just be heartbreaking.'

For more information about Totally Offshore Fishing see:

Totally Offshore Fishing
Deep sea heavy tackle fishing specialists. Reef and light tackle.
Website http://www.totallyfishing.com.au
Email: info@totallyfishing.com.au
Tel: +61 7 3880 2563
Fax: +61 7 3880 2159

Totally Hair Direct
Importers. Distributors. Wholesalers. Hairpieces. Wigs. Synthetic. Real Hair.
Fax: +61 7 3880 2159

Website: www.hothair.com.au

Email: sales@hothair.com.au

Mobile tel: +61 411 365 581

Top Tips

Pete and Shirley offer advice from their own experiences down under:

- Don't be discouraged by rumours that Australians don't like the British. They really are the friendliest people. Even the shopkeepers talk to you as if they've known you for years – they can't do enough for you. Australian life is incredibly child-friendly too. Our kids are able to come everywhere with us and at all the social events we go to there are plenty of activities for them to get involved in while the adults enjoy a glass of Chardonnay.

- Don't be put off by the idea of the heat. Australia is a hot country but it is geared up to cope with that, which makes life much more comfortable. To be out here is far more pleasant in fact than a stifling British summer. Everything is air-conditioned – cars, houses, shopping centres – so there is always somewhere cool to duck. The freezers are super-efficient too. The facilities are such that, as long as you are near civilisation, you can be as hot as you want to be!

- Look carefully into your visa requirements. If you are skilled (i.e. trained in a profession), you may not have to jump through the same hoops as we are having to at the moment. If you have any doubts, seek professional advice. Unless you have a good head for forms, facts, figures and bureaucracy, I'd also advise using an agency to help with your application – it made life so much easier for us and may even have made the difference between getting the initial visa and not getting it.

- Think really carefully about what you are going to take with you; I wish I had brought a lot more with me. You are paying so much for the shipment anyway that you might as well take everything you want. When we moved into our enormous rented house we suddenly realised we had nothing to fill it, none of the homely touches we'd been used to. Of course, leaving things like towels, bedding and mattresses was fine . . . it has been fun replacing all those. Also consider the timing of your furniture removal. We had to live for eight weeks with no home comforts whatsoever. We all ate while sitting on the floor and for a while we slept on the floor too. I wouldn't even let Pete buy mattresses for us because I couldn't be sure they'd fit the beds we were having shipped over – I had to concede in the end, however.

- Don't worry about creepy-crawlies or snakes. The first time I saw a cockroach I went mad and sealed the room for two days before cleaning it from top to bottom. You honestly get used to the bugs – they aren't terrifying! And I haven't seen a single snake in the entire time we've been here.

- When we first arrived, Pete and I were very excited about the cost of living. Australian dollars are weak against the British pound, which makes you think everything is incredibly cheap. Of course, you must remember that you will also be earning in Australian dollars and the salaries here are nothing like as generous as in the UK. The sooner you adjust to the new currency and stop working everything out in sterling, the better.

Budget Sheet

How the Piscinas funded their move and the costs it involved:

The Piscinas were only able to make their move to Australia because they were backed by substantial capital. Although cash flow was sometimes problematic due to delays selling their remaining assets in the UK, Shirley and Pete knew that they had enough to cover their not insubstantial outgoings. Despite the fact that both businesses are now doing well and earning the family a good standard of living, the pressure is still on to meet the tight criteria to enable them to qualify for permanent residency within the next few years.

Practical Directory – Queensland

Region

The Piscinas chose Queensland as their new home. They settled in a town called Scarborough, which is a forty-minute drive north of Brisbane, on the Redcliffe Peninsula near the beautiful Sunshine Coast. Though not as overrun by tourists as the legendary Gold Coast, their stretch has plenty of amenities and enough natural beauty to keep them extremely happy.

Credit	Value (£s)
Sale of family flat and additional land	280,000
Sale of the shop and business	180,000
Savings	30,000
Total	**490,000**

As the state's vibrant capital, Brisbane offers a lively, cosmopolitan ambiance in which to enjoy world-class shopping and cuisine. Closer to home, Redcliffe gives the family all the sun, sea and sand they could possibly ever need, boasting twenty-two kilometres of soft, white beaches as well as wetlands, bikeways and a great family atmosphere.

And should you really want to get away from it all, Queensland's outback is becoming increasingly accessible, offering a fascinating combination of dinosaur relics, wild flowers, sheep-shearing stations, bush pubs and amazing scenery.

Debit	Value (£s)	Value (Aus $)
Business Visa costs	8,000	19,625
Furniture removal	5,000	12,265
Flights	5,000	12,265
Legal fees	2,000	4,906
Boat	170,000	419,640
Fishing equipment	10,000	27,149
Cost of land	133,000	326,265
Projected cost of house build	130,000	318,900
Cost of setting up Totally Hair	50,000	123,000
Cars	12,000	29,515
Other costs (rent, wages, living)	19,000	46,600
Total	**544,000**	**1340,130**

The official tourist guide to Queensland can be found at http://www.destinationqueensland.com, while the Queensland tourist and travel corporations site at http://www.qttc.com.au also provides comprehensive and helpful information.

Culture

The Sunshine Coast, and in particular Scarborough, offers a genuine family atmosphere to all residents and visitors. The Piscinas have found their social lives far fuller than when they lived in Clevedon, with regular barbecues, parties and sports days to attend.

'The great thing about it is that kids are no hassle here, you can take them everywhere,' says Shirley. 'At every gathering the adults drink, eat and chat while all their kids play together in the pool or on the trampoline. Every house becomes an entertainment zone for kids and most have big rumpus rooms for exactly that purpose. Most Sundays we'll have maybe twenty-five or thirty kids at our house, along with their parents. Thankfully, hosting such events doesn't have the same pressure as in England, because everyone brings their own drinks as well as meat to grill on the barbecue.'

Although Australians are laid back and the pace of life is undoubtedly less frenetic than in the UK, they are a very hard-working nation. Courtesy of the fantastic weather and beaches, most free time is spent outdoors engaged in sport, relaxation activities or, of course, barbecuing.

Transport

Queensland is Australia's second biggest state, measuring in at just less than two million square kilometres (around six times the size of the UK). However, to match the state's epic proportions there is a comprehensive and efficient transport system which incorporates 130 domestic airports and a network of around 175,000 kilometres of road.

Travelling by road is a wonderful way to see some of the diverse topography of Queensland and, for people not wanting to stray too far, this method is relatively stress-free. According to Shirley, a four-wheel-drive is mandatory in Queensland as it gives easy access to the beach and other wilderness areas.

Of course, given the vast distances involved, a car isn't

always a practical way to travel in Australia. Shirley regularly takes domestic flights to attend business appointments. For international travel, there are airports in Brisbane, Cairns, Townsville and on the Gold Coast. Queensland also boasts impressive long-distance train routes.

Jobs

The Department of Employment and Workplace Relations (DEWR) is the Australian government agency with prime portfolio responsibility for monitoring skill shortages. The DEWR assesses skill shortages in many ways, including contacting and monitoring employers, industry, employer and employee organisations and education and training providers. At the time of writing the following were among those professionals listed on the skills shortage list for Queensland: childcare professionals, accountants, registered nurses, various health specialists, including dentists and pharmacists and secondary school teachers. There was also a need for practitioners of the following trades: engineering (motor and electrical), electricians, carpenters, bricklayers and decorators, chefs, printers and hairdressers. For updated, more detailed information please visit http://www.workplace.gov.au.

House Prices

Australian interest rates are (at the time of writing) at their lowest point for a generation and this has encouraged increasing numbers of people to jump on the housing ladder. Accordingly, the Australian property market has gone through the roof in recent years and the Sunshine Coast in particular has enjoyed phenomenal property price increases of between 100 and 200 per cent. Allotments (plots of land) are in high demand and whereas in 2001 you might have paid A$60–70,000 (£26–30,000) for one, they are now commanding price tags of around A$200,000 (£86,000). Similarly, the flurry of activity in the building sector has meant that it is not uncommon to wait up to six months for a builder to be able to start work on your dream home.

A typical Sunshine Coast home would be a four-bedroom new-build property, with a formal lounge and dining area, a family/rumpus room and a double garage. In keeping with the outdoor way of life enjoyed there, an outdoor entertaining area is mandatory and usually incorporates a barbecue. On average this sort of property might cost A$370,000–A$420,000 (£158,000–£180,000); a pool would take an additional A$20,000 (£8,500).

Tax

The Australian tax year runs from 1 July and their tax system is based on self-assessment. Each year you must fill out a compulsory annual return, which is subject to a seven-year periodic audit.

Australian income tax brackets run as follows:
    A$0–6,000: not taxable
    A$6,001–20,000: 17 per cent
    A$20,001–50,000: 30 per cent
    A$50,001–60,000: 42 per cent
    A$60,001 plus: 47 per cent

NB: Only income between the brackets is charged at the

applicable tax rate. For example, if a person's income was A\$25,000, only the amount over \$20;001 would be taxed at 30 per cent.

Residency

As you may have inferred from the Piscinas' visa ordeal, getting Australian residency is no picnic. Qualification for a permanent residency visa is assessed on a points system, which takes into account factors such as age, English language ability, specific work experience and whether or not you have any relatives living in Australia.

The points system has a pass mark – a figure at which your application will be assessed. There is also a pool mark – a figure at which your application will be held for two years in case the pass mark drops sufficiently for your application to be considered. These two figures change regularly, so be sure to contact the Australian High Commission or an immigration agency for further information if you plan to make an application. Application forms, general information about immigration policies, categories and requirements can also be found on the main website of the Australian Department of Immigration & Multicultural & Indigenous Affairs (DIMIA) at http://www.immi.gov.au. DIMIA's UK & Republic of Ireland office is located at:

Migration Branch
Australian High Commission
Strand
London WC2B 4LA
Website: http://www.australia.org.uk

If you are going to use an agent to help with your visa application, it is recommended that you use one registered with MARA (Migration Agents Registration Authority) as they will be properly regulated and bound by a code of conduct. Shirley and Pete Piscina used the following:

> Four Corners Emigration
> Strathblane House
> Ashfield Road
> Cheadle
> Cheshire
> SK8 1BB
> United Kingdom
> Tel: + 44 (0) 161 608 1608
> Fax: + 44 (0) 161 608 1616
> Email: info@fourcorners.net
> Website: http://www.fourcorners.net

There are four main types of Residence Visa:

SKILLED MIGRATION

If you have post-secondary qualifications and are under 45, this may well prove your best way of entering Australia. In order to qualify for Skilled Migration residency, your nominated occupation (the one in which you are qualified and have experience) must appear on the Australian Skilled Occupations list. This list can be accessed on the Internet and alters on a monthly basis according to current demand.

In addition to having a required occupation, you will need to speak good English, provide evidence of relevant recent work experience and will be subject to a skills assessment by the Australian assessing authority designated to your nominated occupation. Other factors such as your financial situation and spouse's skills will also be considered.

If you have family members resident in Australia it is possible for them to sponsor you and will add further points to your application.

BUSINESS OWNER

The Business Visa has changed since the Piscinas applied. They got to Australia on a 457 Visa which no longer exists. To apply for the current Business Visa you must:

- Be under 45 years of age

- Speak vocational English

- Possess an overall successful business career or business background

- Have ownership interest in a business of at least 10 per cent

- Have total net assets of A$500,000 (which you are able to transfer across in two years) plus sufficient assets of around A$50,000 to settle

- Have total assets in the business for the past two out of four years prior to applying of A$200,000

- Have a company turnover for the last two out of four fiscal years of A$500,000

- A viable business proposal

- A clean bill of health and a clear criminal record.

Meeting these criteria satisfactorily will gain you a four-year temporary visa. In order to gain permanent residency you will need to apply within that four-year period, ensuring that your Australian business has achieved the following:

- Been in business for at least two full years

- In the twelve months prior to your application the business must have turned over at least A$300,000

- Employed two staff full-time for twelve months prior to the application

- Remains a viable business proposal

You must have:

- Net assets in the business of A$100,000 for twelve months prior to the application

- Total net assets of A$250,000 for the twelve months prior to the application (this can include the A$100,000 in the business)

- A clean bill of health and a clear criminal record.

BUSINESS – SENIOR EXECUTIVE

This is the only option open to businesspersons who have not actually owned their own business. To qualify, you must:

- Be under 45 years of age

- Have occupied a senior management role on the top three levels for between two and four years

- Have a company annual turnover of A$50,000,000

- Have total net assets of A$500,000 (which you are able to transfer across in two years) plus sufficient assets to settle

- Have a realistic commitment to establish a qualifying business (qualifying criteria include that the Australian business has been running for two years, that it has had a twelve-month turnover of A$300,000, that you have net assets in the business of A$100,000 and total personal net assets of A$250,000 and that the business employs two full-time Australian citizens).

SPONSORSHIP

These criteria are similar to those required for the Business Visa but if you get sponsorship the amount of funding you need comes down, and the age limit increases to 55. Sponsorship can also make the targets for your Australian business less stringent. In short, getting sponsorship makes things an awful lot easier!

In order to get sponsorship you will need to apply directly to the government of the region you wish to live in. You tell them what your business plan is and, if they think it will be of benefit to the region's economy, they will sponsor you. It is easier to get sponsorship in the less densely populated areas of Australia; Adelaide is a good one to try. Due to the volume of people wanting to move to Australia, getting sponsorship in Queensland is nigh on impossible.

There are a number of other visas available for applicants including the Retirement Visa and the new Contributory Parent Visa. Please see the contacts in this section for further details.

All of the above visas will provide you with residency. Australian citizenship can be obtained if you have lived in the country for two years and sit, and pass, the citizenship exam.

Please note that visa requirements are updated regularly. The criteria listed here are correct at the time of writing but can only act as a guide. In order to find any changes to the criteria please check with the contacts listed at the beginning of the Residency section.

Education

As you might expect, Australia has a well-developed state education system not dissimilar to that found in the UK. Participation rates and secondary school completion rates are among the highest in the world.

The Federal Government is responsible for national policies and strategies for education, although their actual delivery is the preserve of the individual States and Territories and therefore small differences may occur in schooling. Both levels of government share responsibility for the funding and administration of education.

A year of pre-school education for children aged four or five is available, though not compulsory, in Australia. Despite this preparatory year not being a legal requirement, take-up is almost universal. In order to enrol your child at the local state pre-school you will need to place their name on the waiting list. At the enrolment interview you will need to take proof of the child's date of birth with you.

Primary school lasts either six or seven years depending on the State or Territory. In Queensland, where the Piscinas live, children start aged five or six and complete seven years

Martin Kirby and Maggie Whitman –
from Norfolk to Catalonia

Debbie and Alastair Johnston –
from London to the Chamonix Valley

Kevin Snuggs and Carol Hill –
from Banstead to Brittany

Pete and Shirley Piscina –
from Clevedon to Queensland

Craig Balmain and Sasha McFadyean –
from Hampshire to the Sierra Aracena

Laura and Mac McKay –
from the Chiswick suburbs to the valleys of Provence

(*above*) William and Miranda Taxis – from Hereford to Tuscany
(*below*) Andie and Marie Cox – from Hereford to Vrouhas

Benn and Amy Coley –
from London to Landes

of primary education before moving on to secondary school. Your child can be enrolled at a local school simply by contacting the school directly.

Wherever you are in Australia, school education is compulsory until the age of fifteen (Year 10). At the end of this year the pupils of state secondary schools will receive a Year 10 certificate showing the student's level of achievement in each subject studied. After this, there is usually the option to do two years of additional non-compulsory senior education up to Year 12. Upon completion of this, pupils will receive a Student Education Profile that includes a Senior Certificate detailing individual subject results and, if applicable, a Tertiary Entrance Statement for entrance to university. In Queensland, students requiring a Tertiary Entrance Statement must sit the statewide Queensland Core Skills Test at the end of Year 12. The test is based on the Queensland senior curriculum and is taken regardless of subjects studied.

Further education (or tertiary education) in Australia can be divided into two quite distinct types. Higher education programmes are usually offered by universities and will normally result in Bachelor degrees or a similar postgraduate award. There is also the option to enter into the competency-based Vocational Education and Training (VET) sector, which offers a huge selection of programmes under the National Training Framework.

Although tuition fees were abolished in 1974, legislation governing their implementation has been gradually liberalised and now many institutions will charge fees for some of their places. To finance higher education the government also introduced the Higher Education Contribution Scheme (HECS) in 1989, which covers around 35 per cent of the tuition costs. HECS may either be paid each semester or deferred until the student's income exceeds a stated level.

Parallel private education institutions exist in every State and Territory and play a huge role in the education of Australia's youth – some 30 per cent of children attend them. The majority of non-government schools are Catholic and, in fact, all three of the Piscinas' children attend a private Catholic school at the end of their street.

'Both Pete and I and the kids are really happy with the school they are attending,' smiles Shirley. 'It only costs around £600 (A$1470) a term for all three of them, making it much cheaper than private schools in England.'

School hours are more or less the same as those in Britain but the school year runs from late January or early February until early December.

Health

Australian residents enjoy a world-class health care system in terms of both its efficiency and functioning. The system involves both public and private health care providers and aims to ensure an affordable or free health scheme for everyone in Australia.

The main part of the national health care system is called Medicare – the universal health insurance scheme. It is funded largely through general tax revenue and, more explicitly, through a specific Medicare levy based on an individual's taxable income.

Medicare provides:

- access to free treatment as a public (Medicare) patient in public hospitals

- free or subsidised health care by practitioners

- subsidised prescribed medicine

Medicare does not cover things such as dental examinations and treatments, glasses or contact lenses, medicines and medical services which are not clinically necessary.

Many people in Australia opt to take out private insurance to fill the gaps not covered by Medicare. This course of action is actively encouraged by the Federal Government, who realise the private sector's important contribution to the viability of the Australian health care system as a whole. As an incentive towards private health insurance the Government provides a 30 per cent subsidy and has also introduced other measures to promote long-term participation in a private health scheme.

Useful Contacts
Property information was supplied by:

> Robert Webber of Webbers First National Real Estate
> 83 Bulcock Street
> Caloundra
> Queensland 4551
> Email: mail@firstnat.com.au
> Website: http://www.Caloundraqld.com.au

CHAPTER 6

From Hampshire to the Sierra Aracena

Craig Balmain and Sasha McFadyean were living separate lives under the one roof of their rented Hampshire home. With their jobs taking over their lives, it was time for some drastic action.

Craig and Sasha first met while working as holiday tour leaders. Both were bright, adventurous and fun-loving, and their chosen careers suited them down to the ground – they loved it. Soon after they moved in together, however, the couple decided it was time to grow up and get more stable 'proper' jobs. With this their stated goal, the couple moved to London, bought a flat and each got a desk job ... but soon after began to find themselves stifled and unstimulated.

'We were both still working in the adventure travel industry,' explains Sasha, 'but it was completely different now. We had a desk, a computer, a phone, and a nine-to-five existence – after leading such active lives it was quite difficult to adapt.'

Nevertheless, the Balmains battled on in the London rat race for four years, at which point Sasha fell pregnant and had the couple's first child, Gordon, followed in due course by Gala, their daughter, thereby changing their lives again.

'From this point on I stayed at home all day with the kids. Craig took a job in Hampshire, so we moved and rented accommodation there. I didn't know a soul in Hampshire and so I found life very difficult. I was on my own a lot and found myself desperately trying to fill my days, which, after doing so much previously, was quite a shock to my system.'

To make matters worse, Craig's new job involved long hours and the occasional weekend in the office.

Craig too realised that their family situation was far from satisfactory. 'My job was in middle-management, I was designing and contracting out holiday packages for a travel company. I'd waited a long time to get a "proper" job – I was well into my thirties – but even then I definitely made the wrong choice. I found it tedious and entirely unfulfilling.'

In addition to hating his job, Craig could see how miserable Sasha was and desperately wanted to spend more time with his children. With their relationship at a low point and both of them unhappy with their lives, the family knew it was time to consider a serious change of direction.

For as long as they had been working behind desks Craig and Sasha had idly talked about going somewhere and involving themselves in the other side of the holiday industry. With so much experience in tourism, wouldn't they be excellent candidates for providing package holidays? These discussions gradually became a little less idle and a little more practical, and Sasha and Craig's excitement grew.

'I thought our existence was awful,' admits Sasha. 'I just couldn't continue that life year in, year out. I wanted to see if we had the means to buy a place of our own somewhere, do it up as a hotel, and then have groups over. I put a lot of pressure on Craig and nagged him desperately. It was easy for me to dream but Craig is a lot more practical and was concerned with how we could do it.'

Craig – a typically cautious Scotsman by his own admission – had reservations about leaving his job and giving up their only income when two small children were dependent on him.

'It was a really difficult decision for me,' he reflects. 'Sasha doesn't think through all the ramifications and, quite frankly, doesn't give a damn about money!'

Fortunately, a timely realisation that the UK property market had done wonders for the value of their London flat reconciled their dreams. Now worth over £80,000 more than they had originally paid for it, the couple would be able to remortgage the apartment to release equity and buy a property overseas outright, while still having the additional security of keeping the flat along with its paying tenants.

With the financial hurdle overcome, and the long-established dream of running a hotel set to become reality, the next decision to be made was: where? As it happens, this was the easy part. Sasha had been brought up in Spain and had lived most of her life in Mallorca; Craig was very familiar with Spain too, after all his years of leading tours, and spoke fluent Spanish to boot. There was little room for dispute.

The couple decided upon Andalucia more specifically. The reasons behind their choice were the simple facts that the tourist season is longer than in most other parts of Spain, and that with plenty of low-budget airlines in the region, tourists would find it easy to get to.

In Autumn 2001 Craig began a series of trips to Andalucia to check out possible locations for their new business. More often than not he was disappointed with the results.

'A lot of Andalucia is very dry and the rest seems to be really expensive,' he laughs. 'There were a few possibilities but nothing had really grabbed me. Sasha and I stumbled upon the area known as the Sierra Aracena in one of the guide books we were reading. A friend of mine also recommended it, so we decided it was worth a visit.'

This time the couple set off together for a ten-day reconnaissance in Spain. The plan was to start in the Sierra Aracena then drive around to some of the other places Craig had marked as potentials.

'As soon as we arrived, we knew this place was the one,' smiles Sasha. 'It was stunning, so verdant and beautiful. Just perfect for our needs really.'

Craig agreed wholeheartedly. 'It is a very Spanish area: no high-rises or swarming tourists, just charming little villages and wonderful countryside. It's easily accessible too and so absolutely ideal for what we wanted to do.'

A frenetic house hunt ensued. Sasha and Craig contacted both of the local estate agents working in the area and trailed them for the next few days looking at dozens of unsuitable properties in the surrounding local villages. They wanted something large, that could house a lot of guests yet fall within their £90,000 budget. On day seven of their ten-day trip, a village house in Castaño del Robledo met their criteria exactly.

The property was certainly large and, although old, it was structurally sound. It would need work, however. At the back of the house was a huge, empty, double-storey shell that needed to be transformed into habitable living space. Once this area had been converted and integrated with the rest of the property, the couple planned to install nine double guest rooms, six with en-suite bathrooms, and a further two bathrooms serving the remainder of the rooms. With a little coercion from Sasha and her mother, who had joined them from Mallorca to offer a second opinion, Craig signed the papers for the house that day and left the deposit with the agent. The hunt was over.

'I know people could accuse us of being reckless and irresponsible,' admits Craig. 'We hadn't thought through the finances properly, we just knew we probably had enough to buy the house. To be honest, I surprised myself, but there comes a point when you just have to go for it. It all starts to fit into place and you just have to take that leap. No matter how organised you are you can't account for everything. We just did it, and although it was rash, we have never looked back.'

With the contract signed, the Balmains had three months' breathing space in which to organise their finances. Fortunately this all rolled like clockwork. As anticipated, Craig was able to remortgage the apartment in London and release sufficient funds to buy the house. It was theirs.

There was now precious little to keep them in England so they gave up the tenancy on their Hampshire home, Craig handed in his notice, they said their final farewells and, on a cold, rainy night in October 2002, Craig, Sasha, Gordon and Gala set off on the long drive to their new home in Spain.

The family's first winter in Spain was pretty dire. Once they had purchased the property, the Balmains were left with nothing but an overdraft to live on. Craig had secured a loan from a Spanish bank to cover the cost of the work that needed doing to the house, and had anticipated that the funds would be available to him in October. Sadly, his calculations hadn't factored in additional time for the legendary Spanish bureaucracy, and in December there was still no sign of the loan.

'It was such a frustrating time,' says Sasha. 'We were just sat, penniless, waiting to be able to put our plans into action. We had anticipated being up and running by March 2003, five months after our arrival, but it soon became apparent that this was not going to happen. The house was sound but it was old and very draughty; I was constantly trying to stop up gaps in doors and windows to keep the kids warm. It was a boring time too: we were living off our credit cards and couldn't go out at all.'

'It was ludicrous,' concludes Craig. 'The loan, which was straightforward enough, took over five months from application to receiving the money ... I just couldn't have anticipated that. It wasn't from the lack of trying on our part either, it is just the way that Spanish banks work. We finally received £40,000 in February. I had applied for more but the garden hadn't been listed on the deeds for our house so, as far as the bank was concerned, it wasn't worth as much as I had claimed. We quickly realised that to get the garden added onto the deeds might take years, so we cut our losses and accepted the smaller amount.'

The one shining success to boost them that bleak winter was Gordon and Gala's rapid adaption to their new life and home. They coped brilliantly, settling into school quickly, picking up the language and becoming good friends with the other village children.

'Although many of the reasons for the move were to do with Sasha and me and the business, of course the kids were considered too,' says Craig. 'We had discussed Spain many times and knew the place would be great for them. England is so bad for kids, people just don't give them time. There is a general attitude that children should be quiet or with a babysitter. Spain has got it so right as far as I'm concerned, because life revolves around kids and everyone loves them, even when they're playing noisily – which is what kids do. They are welcome in restaurants and bars, at parties; everywhere we go. They have so much more freedom and they can play for hours without Sasha and me supervising them, because we know somebody in the village will be looking out for them. Equally, we delight in being able to play with, and talk to, other people's kids without being frowned upon. The village school is basic and small, but perfectly adequate for the needs of a three-year-old and a five-year-old.'

Unable to sit idly and anxious to get the ball rolling with the business, Craig filled the dark winter months by beginning to sort out the finer details of the holidays they would be offering from their hotel. Prior to leaving his job, his boss had agreed to feature Craig's holidays in his brochure. With a copy deadline looming, some serious research and planning was required because Craig had to design and cost his products. There was plenty of exploring to be done in order to find the best walks and the most beautiful scenery. Local stables (from which they could hire horses) needed to be researched, as well as locating and costing restaurants, cafés and transport which would all be used by their guests. Every little thing needed to be considered so that Craig could offer a price agreeable to both himself and travel-bound adventurers.

When the brochure was published with details of what the Balmains were offering, it wasn't long before the phone started ringing with enquiries, and even their first booking for the summer. Despite having done none of the work necessary on the house, Craig was unwilling to turn away business and readily accepted the booking. Getting their hotel (Posada del Castaño) ready was now going to be a race against time.

The delay in receiving the loan had already pushed the schedule back five months and the family's builder, Manolo, wasn't able to begin the work until February 2003. Having planned to do the Balmains' project earlier, by this time he had several additional jobs on and was unable to devote all his time, or manpower, to Sasha and Craig's dream.

'There were four builders in Manolo's team,' explains Sasha. 'But because there were other jobs on, from March onwards we only had two builders working solidly. Sometimes no one at all turned up and we had awful days sitting around knowing no work was being done. We had to hassle Manolo until we got all his builders sent over here; it was frustrating but we did realise it wasn't his fault. We did a hell of a lot of the work ourselves too, far more than the programme showed! We painted, varnished, rubbed down, cleaned and tiled. It was back-breaking work.'

And still they were not in any fit state to accommodate guests when their first booking from England came over in June. In spite of all their hard work, Sasha and Craig had no choice but to put their guests up in other hotels. Financially this was disastrous – they barely broke even. It also meant that for each excursion, Craig had to spend the first hour driving around the villages collecting his guests, and Sasha was left cleaning up after all of them with the kids in tow. This was not how it was meant to be.

At the end of the week the guests left happy, but Sasha and Craig were far from it. A further two bookings were dealt with in this way and it was not until late August that the Posada came close to being finished. With just two weeks until their next booking arrived in September, it was noses to the grindstone in order to avoid a repeat performance.

'The deadlines put huge pressure on us,' says Sasha. 'We were just busy all the time and barely spoke to each other. We simply had to get on with things and that meant neglecting the kids and each other; we didn't communicate and got very frustrated. It was an enormous strain on our relationship and we bickered constantly. I wanted to scream, there was so much tension. At one point I decided I wasn't going to break my back just to get it all done in time and that I would do it in my own time instead. I was feeling horribly guilty about being up a ladder all day and ignoring the kids, who then started misbehaving just because they needed attention. Craig was adamant though that he really wanted to get it done, to be honest, I did too, and we both wanted it to be good.'

The format of the holiday for September's set of guests was different from the previous bookings they had accepted. The first two weeks were to be spent in Seville, Granada and Córdoba, where Craig would act as tour guide; then, for the third and final week the group would come back to Posada del Castaño for some country air. Craig had no choice but to leave Sasha with the kids and the mammoth task of finishing the house.

Faced with one last push Sasha threw herself into it, regularly working till 2 a.m. It seemed an impossible task, but when Craig returned with the guests a fortnight later, the house was finished and, what's more, it looked fantastic. Both Craig and the guests were blown away by Posada del Castaño, and Sasha was finally able to sit down with a cup of tea.

Since those stressful and tense weeks, life has improved dramatically for Sasha and Craig. With the house finally finished it seems the biggest hurdle has been passed.

'We are so much more relaxed now,' smiles Sasha. 'We have found a lot more time and energy to put into our children and each other, and we have even started having fun together again.'

After their first guests departed, the family had a few spare weeks to do the last nips and tucks on the house before opening their doors to the tourists from Seville who descend on the Sierra Aracena in autumn each year to pick mushrooms.

'We don't just do the package holidays, we also operate as a hotel. This is a lot easier, to be honest. We only have to worry about bed-and-breakfast,' Sasha continues.

'We are still penniless,' laughs Craig. 'But the future is looking bright. Our village (which we chose more through luck than judgement) was on the cusp of becoming desirable as a place to live and holiday in when we bought the hotel. A year on, property prices have risen considerably, and there are new facilities opening here. We are situated right in the heart of a Natural Park so our surroundings are beautiful but also very accessible. I have been in the tourist game a long time and there is nothing that tells me this won't work. The way the market is moving at the moment, the way the area is becoming more known and developed, it all points to this venture being a success.'

The family have certainly come a long way since those early battles. On a personal level they spend more time together, have rekindled the spark their relationship used to contain, and now the business side looks set to follow. The anticipated future is so rosy that Sasha and Craig have made tentative plans to finally sell their flat in London and buy another property in the village.

'We think we'll probably buy the house that shares our courtyard,' says Sasha. 'It would be nice to have our own living quarters. All the rooms we have, we rent, so they are all very impersonal hotel rooms. Whenever we have a booking we, or the kids, have to change rooms. I would like my own space and I know Gordon and Gala would too. They need a proper children's room that they can cover with horrid posters and paint with moons or something!'

'It is very hard to have regrets because, to be honest, it was such a desperate move,' says Craig. 'I wish I could see more of my parents and I know they would love to spend more time with the kids. Of course we miss friends too, but on serious reflection we couldn't be happier ... and that goes double for the kids.'

Craig Balmain and Sasha McFadyean's beautifully converted guest house, Posada del Castaño, can be booked for walking holidays, riding holidays or simply as a place to relax. Prices start from €32 per night. Visit http://www.posadadelcastano.com or call +34 959 465502 for details.

Top Tips

Sasha and Craig offer some tips learned from their own experiences:

- Language is essential. I can't believe people are so brave as to make this sort of move without some knowledge of the language. We are both fluent and we have still had trying times with banks, estate agents and the *Turismo* office.

- Relax. You soon learn that you can't be too controlling about things when undertaking a project like this. The Spanish '*mañana*' lifestyle can be really trying when you are under pressure to get things done. Don't get stressed, you will have to live with a lot of upheaval.

- If you are having a substantial amount of work done, you have to have a good relationship with your builders, otherwise they won't work well or simply won't turn up. Our tips for keeping Spanish builders happy is to give them a lot of attention – they love it!

Compliment their work, take an interest in what they are doing, make them cups of tea, offer to hold the torch . . . anything! We found a good cop/bad cop routine worked well. While one of us (the female contingent is generally advisable) exercised every bit of charm we had on them, the other was stern and looked after the financial side as well as keeping the time pressure on. The combination was very effective.

- With young children, you have to think very carefully about where your priorities lie in terms of education. We are both happy with the small village school our children attend, but that is because we have never placed much emphasis on material gadgets and gizmos in order to teach our children. It is basic, and whatever additional materials are needed we pay for. In terms of extra-curricular activities, your children will be limited in the countryside. A lot of our friends' children in Hampshire are attending art classes, violin classes or tennis classes in the evenings. Their lives seem to be an endless whirlwind of appointments. Of course, those facilities just aren't available in our village and some might find this a bit limiting.

- By all means do your research. You must have an inkling of what you are going to do out there, but don't let other people tell you that's not enough. No matter how prepared you are, at some point you've got to let go and take a huge leap of faith. There are so many things we didn't know before the move – and many things we couldn't have known. Lots of people tried to put us off. You just have to work through these things as and when they arrive. Business plans and budgets do go a long way but it takes more than that. You need your self-confidence and own initiative.

- The banks are appalling. I mean, I hate banks in general – I've never had a positive experience with one – but the service I received when we arrived here was unbelievable. People here expect to suffer and they all seem to shrug it off. Just as a comparison, it took me less than two weeks to remortgage our property in London, but here it took five months of endless phone calls. There are additional frustrations too as you aren't able to speak to someone directly and they often can't tell you what the hold-up is. Nothing can prepare you for how awful it is, the bureaucracy is unbelievable. To date that has been the biggest setback.

Budget Sheet

How Sasha and Craig funded their move:
Sasha and Craig really ploughed everything they had into this venture and by their own admission lived on credit cards and their overdraft for the first few months. The bank loan they took out for the work was extremely late in arriving and was less than they had hoped for, leaving them nothing left over to live on.

Throughout all their struggles they had a small regular income from their rented London flat and, of course, the security of the London property itself which could provide them with essential capital if things went horribly wrong.

Credit	Value (£s)
Equity from remortgaging London property	80,000
Rental income from London flat (per month)	120
Loan from Spanish bank	40,000
Total	*120,120*

They did have to borrow further funds from a friend, but this was secured against a development grant which they have applied for through the Regional Council of Andalucia. They expect to get back some 33 per cent of their total investment costs (not inclusive of the actual purchase price of the property).

They are now planning to sell their London home and buy another Spanish property adjacent to Posada del Castaño in order to have their own living quarters away from the guests. This purchase would also allow them to convert the property into additional letting rooms in the future, should the expansion of the business require it.

Although the Balmains admit things are still a little tight financially, most of the work is done, though there are still a few modifications to make around the Posada in order to comply with local tourism laws. Sasha and Craig are hoping that a summer of bookings will give their bank balance a healthy glow.

Debit	Value (£s)	Value (Euros)
Purchase of Posada del Castaño	84,000	125,500
Property taxes	3,600	5,378
Notary fees and property registration	400	597
Cost of work	40,000	59,755
Mortgage fees	1,400	2,091
Total	**129,400**	**193,321**

Practical Directory –
Andalucia – Huelva Province

Region

Huelva is Andalucia's westernmost province and sits on the Portuguese border. Its Atlantic coastline, the Costa de la Luz, is often described as the Spanish Algarve and boasts long, unspoilt sandy beaches dotted with small resort towns that become overrun with Andalucians in July and August. Largely untouched by the ravages of tourism witnessed on the Mediterranean side of Spain, the province incorporates a high proportion of national parkland including the famed *Doñana* National Park – one of Europe's most important wetlands. The microclimate here is not as hot as those experienced by other parts of Spain, making it the perfect area for outdoor activities. Though winters can get a little too chilly for the beach, a year-round average temperature of around 20 degrees Celsius won't sound bad to many Brits!

Aracena is the main town of northern Huelva and is surrounded by one of the most beautiful landscapes in Spain. The *Parque Natural Sierra de Aracena y Picos de Aroche* comprises striking hills, verdant valleys and wonderful stone-built villages. The area is criss-crossed by an extensive network of walking trails.

If you would like more tourist information on the Huelva Province the website http://www.Andalucia.com is helpful. For more specific information on the Natural Park that Craig and Sasha live within visit http://www.fase1.com.

Culture

Huelva Province, like much of Andalucia, is packed with history. Settled by Phoenicians and Romans, the area was also a Moorish stronghold for nearly five hundred years. Traces of each of these mighty civilisations can still be found in the region today.

This particular corner of Andalucia was also crucial in the life of intrepid explorer Christopher Columbus. It was in La Rabida, just east of Huelva city, that Columbus planned and found backing for his voyage, and he set sail for America from Palos de la Frontera.

The Sierra Aracena also has a strong culinary tradition. The village of Jaburgo is reckoned to be the most famous place in all of Andalucia for the production of *jamon serano*, the cured hams so loved by the Spanish. Several other local villages are also said to produce very high-quality hams and this is attributed to the area's micro-climate, which is ideal for the acorns on which the pigs feed.

Transport

Huelva Province is easily accessed from the UK. The three nearest airports are Seville, Jerez de la Frontera and Faro (Portugal). For cheap flights to all three try Avro (http://www.avro.co.uk). GB Airways flies to Seville (http://www.gbairways.com), Ryanair flies to Jerez (http://www.ryanair.co.uk) and easyJet flies to Faro (http://www.easyjet.com).

There is a good network of roads throughout the Sierra Aracena which are regularly serviced by buses which connect most of the small villages. Rail travel is convenient too: the state-run RENFE line runs from Huelva to Zafra, crossing the Sierra Aracena and making many other stops along the way.

Jobs

Andalucia has the third highest unemployment rate of any Spanish region. The figure is currently running at around 12 per cent, although this percentage is decreasing year on year. Work tends to be seasonal because the main industries of the region are agriculture and tourism, and as a result in summer there is often a shortage of labour, though at other times of the year demand for such work far outstrips supply. There is also a professional need for more veterinarians, translators, lawyers and skilled construction workers.

Recruitment
See Chapter 1

House Prices
The Costa de la Luz has been subject to very little promotion and as a result is not well known by the average UK buyer.

There are also very strict building regulations on the coastline to prevent it following the high-rise fate of its del Sol and Blanca brethren. Prices are considerably lower here than those found on better-known Costas, though values have been rising at similar rates. You would probably be looking to pay £110,000 upwards for a new-build villa with sea view.

Inland properties can be bought far cheaper, though there is increasing competition from other foreign buyers which makes it a harder market to master. If you fancy something similar to the type of property taken on by Sasha and Craig, you should probably arm yourself with a budget of around £150,000 – though of course bargains can still be found if you put in the legwork.

Tax
See Chapter 1

Residency
See Chapter 1

Education
See Chapter 1

Craig was amazed to learn that their local village school had a set curriculum for children aged three to six. Gala started when she was two and, despite Craig's doubts, she is really enjoying it.

Health
See Chapter 1

Craig was very impressed with the local health care and confesses that a couple of his guests have had to pay a visit to the nearby hospital.

'It is really impressive, even more so when you consider what a rural location it's in,' he says. 'The hospital itself is brand-new so everything is immaculate. The professionalism and standard of care is excellent and it is so speedy too. The doctors sit waiting for patients to come in!'

Useful Contacts

Much of the information on these pages has come from EURES – the European Job Mobility Portal. For more information on any aspect of living and working abroad, visit their website at http://www.europa.eu.int. There is also a freephone helpline number: 00800 4080 4080.

A lot of information was also provided by Jobcentre Plus, who are part of the EURES network. For more information visit http://www.jobcentreplus.gov.uk or call Jobseekers Direct on +44 (0) 845 606 0234.

Another website that offers handy links for all things Andalucian is http://www.typicallyspanish.com – an independent Spanish search engine and directory.

CHAPTER 7

From the Chiswick suburbs to the valleys of Provence

When Laura McKay settled down on her sofa with a glass of wine to watch *No Going Back* and saw Kevin Snuggs and his family make a go of running a carp-fishing business in Brittany, she decided that her own life could do with a change of direction.

On paper the McKays' existence ticked all the right boxes. Mac was an illustrator for an advertising agency, Laura was an international make-up artist, while their two children Bruno (eight) and Morgan (four) attended a local private school. The family lived in a beautiful semi-detached house in Bedford Park, Chiswick, enjoyed an active social life as well as wonderful annual holidays. What could have been better?

'It sounds really good,' admits Laura. 'Mac and I had great jobs doing creative things, but I couldn't help thinking that there was more to life. We were worked to the bone really; we both did six-day weeks and Mac often worked over seventy hours a week – we barely saw each other. As a mother, I suffered terrible feelings of guilt that I wasn't around for my children enough.

'When I first started thinking about changing things, it was during that awful dull time just after Christmas. I watched an episode of *No Going Back* and just felt so inspired . . . I really thought "we could do that". The final straw came for me when I had a nasty health scare. I found a lump on my breast and it took an agonisingly long time for me to be given the all-clear. Something as profound as that does make you re-evaluate things. Both Mac and I had a good hard look at what our lives were.'

While keen to embrace the idea of change, Mac's nerves were holding him back somewhat. 'I felt it was a big risk,' he says. 'We had two young children dependent on us and, to some extent at least, it really is a case of no going back. Laura and I had great jobs: if we gave them up there would be no chance of getting them back. I did agree with Laura that we needed a change, though. I was approaching forty and was beginning to think about what the rest of our lives might be like.'

Laura and Mac's temptation to contemplate a new life was spurred on by Mac's concern about his children's education. Bruno and Morgan weren't really enjoying their school life. Morgan in particular, being very creative rather than academic, suffered under the strict curriculum and the teaching style didn't really suit her. She was always worrying that she was falling behind the rest of the class and the pressure was starting to take its toll. The McKays had searched their local area for other suitable schools but drew a blank. They realised that for the sake of their children they would need to move to the country or, more appealingly, move to another country. With all the reasons to move abroad piling up into a very convincing case, the family felt it was time to start making some tentative plans.

'The idea of running painting courses had always appealed to me,' explains Mac. 'I did some teaching at my son's school and really enjoyed it. Combined with a lovely destination and accommodation, we realised that it would be a great, and viable, way to make a living.'

The family decided to move to France – a country much loved and visited by them all. It also offered the convenience of being close to the UK, facilitating visits for friends and family, and had the added bonus that Laura and Mac spoke some of the language. To narrow down their property hunt, the couple did some research into the French *départements* to assess their suitability. There were plenty of factors to bear in mind: firstly, location would be all-important in determining how appealing their holidays would be to potential clients. The local climate and scenery had to be considered. Secondly, the McKays also needed to ensure that the place fulfilled their own needs. Moving from London, they weren't convinced that living isolated in the countryside would suit them. They wanted to be near lively cities in which they could enjoy going out and having fun. And, of course, the children needed a good, local, international school that would allow them to flourish and begin enjoying their education again. By the end of their enquiries, their conclusion was simple – they had to move to coastal Provence.

'From my perspective as a painter, and the perspective of the courses, the fact that Provence met all our criteria was a real boon,' Mac enthuses. 'The area has a strong painting tradition; all the great Impressionists spent some part of their lives here. The quality of the light is famous. The mistral keeps the air very clean and free of particles, so the views are fantastic and absolutely crystal clear.'

Having contacted lots of local agents to arrange viewings of suitable properties, Laura and Mac headed to their chosen destination for a seven-day reconnaissance trip. They blitzed the area, visiting over forty properties and getting a feel for the market.

'We didn't really have time to be polite about it,' smiles Laura. 'If we arrived at a property we didn't like, we didn't even bother getting out of the car – that way we could see five in an hour!

'Ironically, the property we ended up buying was the one we visited second. We did really like it when we first saw it, but we didn't have the guts just to go for it. We felt we should see more to make sure we were right, we needed to compare it with others. Most of the others we saw were unsuitable or really expensive, so we came full circle and went to see it again at the end of the trip. Nothing else measured up to it at all.'

With their frenetic house hunt over, and a lot to think about, Laura and Mac returned to Chiswick to discuss everything. To say that they made plans would probably be exaggerating the formality of their discussions, but over a glass of wine or two the couple decided on a few crucial factors. The house was exactly what they wanted. Just twenty-five minutes from the coast and the glamorous cities of Cannes and Nice, yet situated in picturesque countryside surrounded by pretty villages. A twenty-minute drive in the other direction would take them to the mountains and provide the opportunity to ski in the winter. Mac's students would be spoiled for choice deciding which landscapes to paint.

The main property was a three-bedroom house with a galleried master bedroom and a forty-foot lounge. It was surrounded by terraces and had two acres of landscaped gardens in which were a further two guest cottages and a run-down *gîte*. At £450,000 (€672,249), it was more than the McKays had wanted to pay, but they adapted their plans pretty quickly.

'We had originally wanted to buy a property outright, but we reasoned that if we took out a small mortgage the rental income from the *gîte* would eventually cover the payments,' says Mac. 'We calculated that in order to live there comfortably we would need to get ten weeks of holiday courses at full capacity booked each year. That seemed entirely plausible.'

With some of the Is dotted and the occasional T crossed, the McKays put their Chiswick home on the market for £800,000. In such a desirable area, it didn't take long to generate interest and by mid-March they had a potential buyer.

'At about this time we heard from France that there was someone else interested in the house we wanted,' says Laura. 'This news really forced our hand a little and it became apparent that we would have to move quite quickly to secure the house at the price it was on the market for. The Provence/Côte d'Azur area has a very buoyant property market and prices have gone up by about 20 per cent for the last few years. We thought it wouldn't take long for the vendor to increase the price with two parties interested, so we knew we just had to do it. At this time, we hadn't got to the point of exchange on our London home so we literally had to beg, steal and borrow our deposit, which was around £80,000. It was a huge gamble but we were confident of our selling our house because Chiswick is so desirable, particularly Bedford Park, which is the listed bit.'

The couple were arranging a small mortgage through a French bank because the country's interest rates were so low. As no survey was required by the bank in order to secure the mortgage, Laura and Mac took the precaution of hiring a local builder – an expert in stone properties – to look over the house and write a report. Everything seemed to be in order and when the *compromis de vente* (the pre-contract) arrived they took it to their English lawyer to check through. The vendors had used the spectacular property simply as a holiday home for a couple of months each year, and so because it had not been fully inhabited for decades – and because the builder had not had access to some of the property's more technical aspects – their lawyer wisely recommended that they insert a clause into the contract ensuring that the seller guarantee the heating and pool mechanics to be in full working order. The seller agreed and, happy that they had covered their backs, Laura and Mac signed and returned the *compromis*, handing over their substantial deposit.

Although the *compromis de vente* is legally binding, the McKays had a week's 'cooling off' period, during which they could back out of the sale without penalty – with things proceeding smoothly regarding the sale of their own house, however, this was the last thing on their minds. Also within the *compromis* was the agreed date upon which the *acte de vente* (equivalent of completion) was to be signed – in Laura and Mac's case this was scheduled for the end of August. As it was now only April, the family had plenty of time to make their arrangements and begin their goodbyes. It also meant that the elderly gentleman selling the property had time to get the official reports needed to guarantee the heating and pool mechanics. It had been agreed that these reports and guarantees were to be presented upon the day the *acte de vente* was signed.

With the *compromis* back in France, all legal responsibility was passed over to the *notaire* (the French lawyer). Although Laura and Mac were nervous about not having their own representation, they were assured that the normal procedure in France is for the *notaire* to represent both parties during the sale, and indeed this is the case. They reasoned that as this was the norm they would stick with it; after all, with the special clause in the contract they felt pretty confident that not too much could go wrong.

Later that month they took Bruno and Morgan out to visit their new home, and it met with a rapturous response. Rather than their small London garden, the children now had two glorious acres to romp in, as well as their own pool. Weekends could be spent on the beach or skiing in the mountains. The family's excitement grew. By the end of July the final touches were being put on the sale of their Chiswick home. Unfortunately, the process had been subject to delays towards the end, and the date set for completion kept being moved. These hold-ups had a huge impact on Laura and

Mac who were trying to deal with a fluctuating exchange rate. Because the euro was becoming stronger against the pound, every extra day they waited for completion put up the sterling price that they would be paying for their French property. Just two weeks cost them an additional £17,000, a fact which Laura describes as 'a bit of a gutter!'

The family were taking most of their belongings with them to Provence so there was plenty of packing to be done.

'We got everything sorted out,' explains Laura. 'We arranged a moving-in day with the agent and booked our removal van accordingly. We were excited and terrified and unfortunately ran into our first problem before we had even set off! Being typically Mediterranean and not taking business and organisation quite as seriously as perhaps we Brits would, our agent had forgotten to tell the vendor our moving-in date. As a consequence, the old couple had arranged to spend a last couple of weeks in their holiday home at just the time we were supposed to be arriving.

'The agent was very apologetic and to help us out he arranged for our possessions to be stored beneath the house until the vendors left. He even met our removal truck and supervised the unloading. Of course, even with our boxes sorted out, we were still left a bit in limbo because we had moved out of our Chiswick home but couldn't move into our French home. We made the best of a bad situation by loading up our orange VW camper van and spending two glorious weeks driving down slowly through France, stopping anywhere we fancied. It was a brilliant way to start our new life.'

When they finally arrived in Provence, the first job for the

McKays – before even visiting the house – was to sign the *acte de vente* and complete the sale. This rather formal meeting was to be held in the *notaire*'s office and the vendors were also in attendance but, despite their promises and the clause in the contract, they failed to produce the documents guaranteeing the heating and pool mechanics. Bemused, Laura and Mac's first instinct was not to sign, but the *notaire* managed to placate the situation by suggesting that the clause was carried through – the McKays would have the reports done themselves and any problems were to be reported by the *notaire* to the seller who would then pay for repairs. This seemed perfectly reasonable to all around the table and so the final signatures were added to the papers. The McKays now officially owned the beautiful French property they had first seen six months previously.

Apparently overcome with the emotion of selling his beautiful home, the seller declined Mac's kind offer to paint a watercolour of the property for them.

'The old guy we were buying the house off was really sweet and clearly very choked-up,' recalls Laura. 'He appeared to be upset and so I really felt for him. He seemed very proper and nice.'

Sadly, the McKays were about to realise just how deceptive appearances could be. When they finally got out of the *notaire*'s office, they raced to their new home and christened it by leaping in the pool fully clothed. Spirits were high and none of them could have possibly foreseen the sour experiences to come.

Their first days were idyllic; the place felt like home as soon as they had unpacked their boxes. The family enjoyed the sunshine, the pool and eating on the terrace, but it was all quite short-lived and on day three the children were taken to start their new school.

'It was great getting them started straight away after our unusual journey,' says Laura. 'They hadn't had any children to play with for weeks so they loved suddenly being with other kids again. I also felt it was important to establish a routine quite quickly. It was an international school so it wasn't too much of a baptism of fire. After Morgan's experiences of school in England, the last thing I wanted to do was give her another negative image about education.'

With the kids happily installed at school during the days, Laura and Mac were free to begin work on the property and the business – both of which would require substantial effort.

The McKays had set aside a budget of £100,000 (€149,387) on which to live for the first year and which would also cover the renovation work. The main house was entirely habitable so the family were comfortable, but the priority was the guest accommodation – the two cottages would need new bathrooms, kitchens and interiors before Mac's pupils could live in them, and the *gîte* required complete renovation before it could be rented. With no building experience whatsoever and a limited budget, Laura and Mac certainly had their work cut out.

They needed expert help and so they hired the services of Sylvio and his building team, who set to work gutting all the properties and drawing up plans for their new lease of life. While Sylvio got underway, very aware of the time limit imposed by the *notaire* the couple set about organising someone to come and look at the heating and pool plumbing. When their expert came to report back to them, they had a nasty surprise.

'He basically reckoned the pool mechanics had never received a service,' grimaces Mac. 'They were very old and when he turned them on the filter pumped the wrong way. Our beautiful sapphire pool quickly became a murky green. The heating system was even worse: he wouldn't even allow us to turn it on as it looked so dangerous. He thought it would probably leak carbon monoxide, which we were horrified about because the kids' room was just above the boiler. He estimated the cost of repairs would run into thousands of pounds, which we simply didn't have the budget for. We wasted no time contacting the *notaire*.'

But the *notaire* didn't respond. So they contacted him again and forwarded the reports on to him, and still they heard nothing.

At about this time, some more of the property's 'quirks' were uncovered by Sylvio and his team – while fitting the new bathrooms in the guest cottages, it had been noticed that the plumbing was quite unusual. On further inspection, it had transpired that the plumbing was not just unusual but also unhygienic and illegal. No septic tank had been installed for the cottages and all the sewage was running directly out underground. Other aspects of the house were highly unconventional too. The beautiful tiled terraces hadn't been waterproofed and, when the first heavy rains appeared, they leaked a torrential flow of water into the guest rooms below, ruining the fresh plaster and causing the ceilings to cave in.

'Within two months of moving into the house we realised that the seller was not everything we had thought he was,' Mac says. 'There were problems everywhere that had been hidden when we bought the property – we hadn't had a chance of finding all the faults, even with a survey.

'By this time we were calling the *notaire* three times a day and sending letters but we never had a response. We were also learning from local friends about a lot of the corruption which is rife in the area. Although we could never prove anything, we began to suspect that perhaps the *notaire* was in league with the wealthy vendor . . . he certainly didn't seem to want to do anything for us.'

With the bill for these unforeseen problems running to almost £50,000 (€74,693), and the *notaire* apparently unwilling to hold the vendor to the contract, the McKays decided to approach an independent solicitor for advice. Apart from anything else winter was beginning to draw in and their heating system was still dangerously unsafe because they had been advised not to touch it until the vendor had agreed to pay for the repairs.

The last time the *No Going Back* cameras were with Laura and Mac they had reached rock bottom. In order to get to the bottom of the problem, their solicitor had gone to the *Mairie* (town hall) to look over the plans for the house and had discovered a serious discrepancy between what stood on the site and what should have been on the site according to the plans.

'At the point Ricochet finished filming we were very frightened,' Laura recalls. 'We were left hanging for a horrible week, not knowing whether our house was allowed to be where it was. As it happens, it is fine. The problem was that the previous owner had built extensions and add-ons that he hadn't got planning permission for. Apparently that is fairly normal in this region but, had they been there less than ten years, the *Mairie* could have forced us to tear them down. Thankfully, all the additions were done some forty years ago so there was not any case for making us change them back.'

And fortunately from here, things were only going to get better for Laura and Mac. 'The solicitor we saw was one recommended to us by Sylvio, who is now a very good friend of ours,' explains Mac. 'Previously we were at a very low point because we knew a lot of corruption existed and so we thought it might not even be worth going to a solicitor, that he'd just tell us we had to accept the way things were here. Once our solicitor had sorted out the problem with the deeds, though, he quickly reinstalled our faith in the legal process. He reassured us that we did have a case, and not just for the heating and pool mechanics (which had been covered by the added clause in the contract), but also for everything else. Apparently there is a French law called *Vice Cache*, which basically means that the seller cannot hide faults he knows about from the buyer. It looks likely that we can claim for the septic tank and for waterproofing the terracing under this law because the vendor should have told us about these problems when he sold us the place. Our solicitor told us in no uncertain terms that we had a very strong case. As you might imagine, after six months of stress and doubt, we were absolutely delighted.'

With legal proceedings under way and a positive prognosis, Laura and Mac felt like a huge weight had been lifted. They could start to enjoy life again.

Meanwhile, unlike their parents, Bruno and Morgan had found life in France far less stressful than in England. Both had settled into the international school and were thriving under the more relaxed and varied curriculum.

'Morgan in particular just loves it,' says Laura. 'She is given the freedom to think creatively and she is much more relaxed about school. Even though it is an international school we really wanted both our kids to mix with the locals and learn the language, so we were delighted to discover that 30 per cent of the pupils are French and that they are taught French language every day. In addition, both our children do lots of activities in the community. Bruno plays football for the local team three times a week and both of them go to French ski school so they have lots of French friends. I don't think they understand everything yet, but they certainly know enough to get by and understand what is going on.

'They are an inspiration to us really; watching your kids adapt is fascinating. For example, if we go to the beach, even early on before they spoke much French, they would just go up to the other children and communicate in the best way they knew how. It never seemed to make much difference to any of them, they all ended up playing together anyway.'

Obviously the unanticipated problems that came with the house had not been factored into the McKays' budget. Even with court proceedings looming, they are not likely to see financial recompense for some time, so they had to adapt their budget and plans to cater for the unforeseen change in circumstances. In order to cover the costs of installing a new septic tank, of repairing the heating and pool pump and of ripping up and waterproofing the terraces, one of the guest cottages was left untouched for the first year – the family simply did not have the funds to renovate it.

Every other facet of their business plan was coming along

swimmingly, though. The newly created Azur Painting Holidays website was generating lots of enquiries and the occasional booking. The accommodation was taking shape and looking magnificent. And, in an unexpected but welcome turn of events, Sylvio was becoming a very valued family friend as well as the builder.

'I had planned to do a lot of the work myself, but I had no experience of building,' confesses Mac. 'I thought it was going to be far less work than it was. I had anticipated the first cottage taking me fifteen days . . . it took me over thirty! The more problems we ran into, the more we came to rely on and trust Sylvio. At first we had quite a strained relationship – he had lots of strange ideas about the way we should do things, they were very different to ours and he just didn't seem to listen to what we wanted. It's like any friend, though: over time we came to accept our differences and now we work together terrifically and I have an awful lot of respect for him. Whenever I wasn't sure how to do a job, Sylvio would come around at the weekend and do it with me, completely free of charge. When time was running out on the parts of work contracted to his team and they were behind schedule, he put in an incredible amount of overtime and never charged us a penny for it. He is a man of his word and he was determined to get it finished on time. Sylvio is without doubt the nicest bloke we have ever met. I have never known someone do so much for a family of strangers and expect absolutely nothing in return. His wife is the same. We owe them so much.'

Even with all the trials the McKays faced, through their hard work and with the help of their saviour Sylvio, Azur Painting Holidays opened on schedule in April 2003.

With the house and garden looking beautiful, Mac offering top-quality landscapes and teaching and Laura rustling up wonderful Provençal meals for their guests, the holidays were a resounding success for all concerned.

'We really, really, really enjoyed it,' says Laura of their first season of holidays. 'Running the holidays was a nice experience from start to finish. I loved doing the cooking and am really proud of myself because I am self-taught. In all those weeks I never received a single complaint – quite the reverse! Of course Mac took to the painting courses like a duck to water and loves every minute of it.

'We've had some really great people to stay and most of them stay in touch with us. We get cards and photos and emails, which is lovely because then you feel you've done your job. We really try to keep the holidays informal and to make the guests feel like friends who are staying with us, rather than clients.

'It's brilliant when really stressed people arrive for a holiday because then you see the change. Usually they don't talk very much at first and are nervous because they think they aren't very good at painting, but by the third day they chat and come into their own and relax. It is incredibly satisfying and quite often they are different people by the end of the week.'

There is no doubt that Azur Painting Holidays has been a hit. In their first season they were fully booked, and the second season on which they are now embarking boasts equally impressive statistics. The wonderful thing about the McKays' life, though, is that they haven't lost sight of why they moved. The painting holidays only run for ten weeks of the year, although they could undoubtedly take bookings for many more.

'We came here with a very different attitude really,' Laura explains. 'We could run holidays all year round and earn pots of money but that's not what life is about for us. We want to make enough to continue living here ... and we do. More importantly, we want time to spend as a family.'

It is not as though there is nothing to do for the rest of the year: four properties, two acres of gardens and two pools don't look after themselves. Then there's the website to update and the administration to sort out. Mac is also doing his own painting, which he now exhibits both in France and the UK.

The *gîte* that was painstakingly renovated by the McKays last year has exceeded all expectations too. Originally expected to be let for twelve weeks of the year, it has so far been full for twice that.

So, with the family blissfully happy, the business thriving and the house in perfect working order, the only thing still hanging over the McKays is the legal wrangling with the previous vendor, and even this doesn't seem to be getting them down too much any more ...

'He has already tried to settle, so he knows we have a good case,' says Mac. 'We refused his offer, though, because we are so far down the legal road now, we feel we might as well take it all the way ... Besides, it looks like we are entitled to far more than he offered. And if the payout is as healthy as we think it might be, we're going to take Sylvio and his family on holiday to say thank you for all their help. I hear Cuba is nice ...'

If you fancy turning your hand to a bit of painting in the Provençal countryside, or even if you just want to laze by the pool, give Laura and Mac a call on +33 49 34 29 599 or visit www.azurpaintingholidays.com. The self-contained *gîte* within the McKays' grounds, La Calèche, is also available for rent.

Top Tips

Laura and Mac offer some advice for anyone thinking of making a similar move:

- Always get advice from professionals before you do anything. We learned so many important things from our lawyer in England. Inheritance laws in France are very complicated so we sought advice about under whose name we should buy the property, which proved invaluable. We also got professional help in organising our business account from England for the first two years, just until we became a bit more familiar with the French tax system and had made contact with a good accountant out here.

- In order to prevent having your fingers burned the way we did, we would always advise that you have your own notary for the property transaction in France: do not use the same one as the vendor. As charging fees are very strictly regulated, this shouldn't actually cost you any more. We'd also recommend that you get the name of a notary from a party entirely independent of the sale. Try your local school – perhaps they have a recommendation?

- If your children will be attending the local school, try and arrange for them to spend a day or two there before you sign them up. Some schools are very unwilling to accommodate non-French-speaking children, and their reaction to your request should give you some idea of how they feel. Of course, it doesn't happen often, but some friends of ours (also from the UK) had to take their children out of the school they were attending because they were not given any support and were just ignored by the pupils and teachers.

- If you go house hunting in the summer, try and imagine what the property will be like in winter. The sun gets just as low in France as it does in the UK, and in a landscape dotted with valleys this can be problematical. Some friends of ours bought a house that doesn't get any proper daylight for two months of the year. By the time the days get longer again, the property is absolutely covered in moss.

- This is probably easier said than done, but try and check the crime level of the specific area in which your house is situated. People think that because they are in the Provençal countryside their house won't get burgled, but we live very close to the major cities of Cannes and Nice, which have all the same problems of any big city in the world. Where we are is fine, but some friends about a mile away have been broken into twice this year. It is not unheard of for expensive-looking cars to be followed back from the cities by burglars.

- Do not try moving abroad to a new life without a
  decent financial cushion. It's easy to get caught up in
  the idea of moving to a new place and a new life, and to
  ignore the fact that most people will face some
  problems during their move of one kind or another.
  Without a well-thought-out plan and a contingency
  fund of money to cover these eventualities, it not only
  would add to the stress of it all, but could be
  devastating to your plans. Had we not had that large
  back-up fund, we would have run out of money quickly
  and had no way of paying our mortgage or living costs.

Budget Sheet

How Mac and Laura funded their move:
Laura and Mac spent considerable time, and funds, planning
the financial aspects of their move and of setting up the business. They consulted experts and specialists in France and in
the UK to make sure their plans were feasible.

As a result of their prudence the McKays were able to sur-
vive against all odds in spite of the enormous, and
unpredicted, costs incurred while doing up the property.
Without the precaution of professional advice, the McKays
may not have had enough of a financial cushion to soften the
blow, resulting in them being forced to return to the UK.
Happily, their finances were in good order and they were
able to adapt their plans to accommodate the changes. Best
of all, they can look forward to a healthy pay out from the
legal proceedings at the end of the year.

Credit	Value (£s)
Sale of Chiswick property	800,000
Mortgage on French property	100,000
Total	**900,000**

Practical Directory – Provence

Region

Officially named Provence Alpes Côte d'Azur, the administrative region of Provence in France's south-east corner
covers a vast swathe of dramatically varying geography and
is divided up into six *départements:* the wild Alpes de Haute
Provence; the mountainous Hautes Alpes; the pretty Bouches
du Rhône; quaint Vaucluse – home of the Provençal wine
industry and the adventurous Peter Mayle; tourist rich Var; and,
finally, the Alpes Maritimes – part of whose mountainous
coastline forms the infamous and glitzy Côte d'Azur.

Arguably, the true heart of Provence can be found in the
hills between the dramatic extremes on either side. It is in
these foothills, overlooking the Loup Valley, that Laura and

Debit	Value (£s)	Value (Euros)
Mortgage to be paid off on Chiswick property	200,000	298,776
Cost of French property	450,000	672,246
Associated cost of buying property	36,000	53,779
Moving costs	5,500	8,217
Renovation costs	100,000	149,400
Cost of remedying problems left by vendor	50,000	74,700
Total	*841,500*	*1257,118*

Mac bought their home. Although they live surrounded by peaceful scenery, they are actually just a twenty-five-minute drive from the glamorous cities of Nice and Cannes. They can also indulge in one of their favourite family activities – skiing – in beautiful Isola 2000 (one hour away) or even closer in Gréolières-les-Neiges (twenty-five minutes away).

Provence also benefits from a good climate, boasting long, hot summers, warm springs and autumns and mild winters where snow or frost are rare.

For further tourist information see www.francetourism.com or www.franceguide.com; for more specialised details about Provence, try www.provenceweb.fr.

Culture
Provence was catapulted to fame by Peter Mayle's novel *A*

Year In Provence and has remained a firm favourite with Europeans and Americans ever since. It is a beautiful part of the world, renowned for fields of lavender, terracotta roof tiles and yellow ochre colourings. These colourings were traditionally brought in by the spice boats and have been used to decorate local houses both internally and externally ever since.

For centuries the landscape – and famous light – has captured the hearts and inspired the minds of world-famous artists; Cézanne, Van Gogh and Chagall all have links with the region. Still very much a centre for the arts, Nice boasts a spectacular outdoor jazz festival, while, more famously, Cannes becomes the focus of the film world once a year. Among the many culinary and gourmet delights to emerge from this region, probably the most celebrated is the Provençal wine. The Côtes du Rhône appellation is grown in the vineyards south and west of Orange, while Châteauneuf-du-Pape is produced in the area around the eponymous medieval village.

Transport

Laura and Mac are based just a twenty-five-minute drive from Nice international airport which is regularly serviced by flights from most UK destinations. Try easyJet (www.easyjet.com) for cheap flights. British Airways (www.british-airways.com), British Midland (www.flybmi.com) and Air France (www. airfrance.com) might also be worth investigating. Toulon and Marseille Provence airport also offer access to the region.

The Eurostar travels direct to Avignon, from where it is possible to get a train to almost any major town. Rail travel is excellent along the coast and in the Rhône valley as these areas are serviced by fast and frequent trains. The slower but scenic Train des Pignes connects the coast (at Nice) with Digne les Bains in the heart of the Alpes de Haute Provence – the entire journey takes about three hours.

Jobs

The Provence Alpes Côte d'Azur has an unemployment rate of around 11.5 per cent – higher than the national level. Ironically, there is also a high, unmet, labour demand in many sectors. Recruitment problems are endemic here, and it is a qualitative mismatch between supply and demand that is to blame. Examples of industries short of skilled labour include: distribution, construction and transport.

Recruitment

See Chapter 2

House Prices

Provence is legendarily popular with the overseas property buyer, making it one of the most expensive places in Europe to buy a home. Demand is high and has pushed prices up to massively inflated levels, with some agents advising not to pin any hopes on the exclusive Provence locality with a budget of less than £250,000 (€373,450). Although bargains can still be found, they are few and far between. Most crumbling farmhouses have already been snapped up and renovated, and even if you are lucky enough to stumble upon one, be warned that they can be costly to restore . . . Before signing on the dotted line plant your feet firmly back on the ground and make sure your pockets are deep enough at least to install running water.

If you have got the budget to get a foot on the Provençal

property ladder, it is well worth the plunge. Typical homes in the region are beautiful – either elegant village houses featuring roof terraces or courtyards, or stone *mas* (farmhouses, usually with many outbuildings, vineyards and olive groves). Prices for a small village house away from the sea and with a roof terrace might start from £100,000 (€149,385), whereas a large *mas*, luxuriously appointed with extensive grounds and a swimming pool, will cost at least £750,000 (€1,120,390). The most expensive area in Provence is close to Les Alpilles, les Baux, St Rémy de Provence and Aix-en-Provence, while the area tipped for best value for money is close to the border of Languedoc-Roussillon.

Tax
See Chapter 2

Residency
See Chapter 2

Education
See Chapter 2

Health
See Chapter 2

Useful Contacts
Information in this section relating to jobs has come from EURES – the European Job Mobility Portal. For more information on any aspect of living and working abroad visit their website at http://www.europa.eu.int. There is also a freephone helpline number: 00800 4080 4080.

Information was also supplied by property agents:

VEF (UK) Ltd
4 Raleigh House
Admirals Way
London
E14 9SN
Tel: +44 (0) 20 7515 8660
Fax: +44 (0) 20 7515 5070
Email: info@vefuk.com
Website: www.vefuk.com

CHAPTER 8

From Herefordshire to Tuscany

When William and Miranda Taxis made their New Year's resolutions on the eve of the Millennium, they found themselves taking the decision to change their lives for good.

It can hardly be denied that the Taxis family love a challenge. The couple's lovely Herefordshire home, where they lived with their two young daughters Isabella and Annie, had been bought as a shell and gradually, lovingly reconstructed. William, a builder, and Miranda, a teacher, had put heart and soul – not to mention back-breaking labour – into the place and five years on it was nearing completion. With an idyllic house worth around a quarter of a million pounds and no mortgage, the couple could have been sitting pretty but, instead, they decided they wanted to move.

'I know it sounds crazy,' laughs Miranda, 'but we just fancied a new project. We didn't want to sit around and watch life go by, and we were so comfortable in Herefordshire we could have stayed there for ever. So, during a life-changing discussion on Millennium morning, we decided to move house that year.

'What also fuelled this decision was the fact that we were in a great position to make a change in our lives: we were essentially free to do whatever we wanted within the value of our house. Our daughters were very young and we had no debts or mortgage.'

And so the idea was born.

The Taxis' initial plan was to find another house in need of restoration and do it up while living in it. William was keen to move up the property ladder and so the hunt for a bigger, better house to renovate got under way. In spite of their best efforts, and a not inconsiderable budget, William and Miranda drew a blank. They could not find anything that caught their eye or tugged at their heartstrings.

'The only properties that we really liked or that we could really see the potential in we would have needed a mortgage to buy, and that's before funding any of the work,' explains William. 'The UK property market was just beyond our means, so we decided to look overseas.'

The couple narrowed their choices down to France or Italy, a decision based primarily on language; William spoke excellent French and being half-Italian was accordingly fluent.

'The deciding factor was really the property market,' William admits. 'Both France and Italy are beautiful countries and we were sure we could make a new start in either, but in Italy it seemed to be possible to buy a wonderful, historic property, which was in need of work, reasonably cheaply. We also knew that once the restoration was complete the market was strong enough for us to be able to sell it on for a very good price. Basically, Italy offered us the chance to make an excellent return on our investment.'

A new hunt began. William and Miranda combed the Internet and risked the vagaries of Italian estate agents in a quest to find their new home. They took regular trips out to Italy to view properties – a task made nearly impossible by the apparent ineptitude of some of the estate agents they dealt with.

'We generally dealt with small, local agents and had quite a few memorable experiences,' recalls Miranda. 'They would frequently forget to come and meet us, or mislay the piece of paper they had written our details on . . . On occasion they didn't even have the keys to get into the properties we wanted to see. It is just a different way of doing things here, and there is no point in trying to change it; you have to keep a sense of humour about everything. Our funniest moment was probably when we went to see a hilltop house in Chianti. Our agent had offered to drive us, but the problem was that he couldn't remember how to get to it. The most frustrating thing was that because the property was on such high ground we could all see it! We spent about an hour circling the house and in the end he had to call a friend and wait for him to arrive and lead us there.'

Throughout the remainder of 2000, the Taxis methodically scoured the Italian countryside with infinite patience for a suitable property. William's mother – a native Italian with lots of Italian friends – was also drafted in to help with the quest. It was she who, in February 2001, put William and Miranda in contact with Orietta Bono, who was selling a farmhouse property in the Tuscan village of Rigutino, near Arezzo. On paper the house was a hot contender, so the couple wasted no time booking flights to Pisa to go and view the property.

'Orietta and her son took us to see the farm and William and I were driven in separate cars,' smiles Miranda. 'We had to travel down a long, dusty road to get there and en route we passed the most magnificent house that really caught my eye. Strangely enough, William had noticed it from his car too. The property we were going to see was actually on the neighbouring land and when we arrived it was clear it wasn't suitable. During Orietta's tour of the farmhouse the only thing that really interested either of us was the window from which we could see the other beautiful house.'

William and Miranda couldn't help themselves and asked if the neighbouring property they could see was for sale and if she knew who was selling it. Amazingly they discovered that it was indeed available and that Orietta herself was the vendor.

'She hadn't taken us to see it because it was priced substantially above our budget of £200,000,' says William, 'but when she saw how taken with it we were she agreed to show us around. When we arrived at the other house, Il Pero (The Pear Tree), we knew our search was over. We felt like we had just found a diamond.'

Il Pero was a vast Leopaldina estate farm house built in 1782 and came complete with original kitchen the size of a banqueting hall, around twenty rooms, two acres of land and lots of outbuildings. Majestic and full of character, it had, none the less, been empty for decades and was sorely neglected. Although in parts fairly structurally sound, the roof leaked, there was no running water or electricity and half of it was near ruin, having been occupied by animals. It would need a huge amount of work and investment, and the price tag was £270,000 (€403,325).

Leaving their hearts in Italy, the Taxis returned to England and did their sums. They couldn't make a move on Il Pero until they had substantial capital, as the vendors required a large deposit. In Italy this is normal procedure and usually clocks in at around 30 per cent of the asking price.

The Herefordshire house went on the market at £260,000 and all Miranda and William could do was wait, and hope. But the wait was a long one. Their home took nine nail-biting months to sell.

'Our first estate agent really messed up,' grimaces William. 'A couple who were interested in buying the house asked for details almost straight away but were told that there weren't any yet available and were never sent any at a later date. When we transferred to another agent six months later, the same couple came across the house again. They ended up buying it at the full asking price in January 2002. It is frustrating to think that without that incompetence from our first agents, we could have sold it six months earlier and been able to buy Il Pero in April 2001.

With the sale completed, the Taxis family moved into rented accommodation and made plans for the start of their new life. All of their belongings were being taken over to Tuscany, so a mammoth packing session was required. Their possessions were to be gradually moved to a local warehouse over the course of five days so that the removals lorry could be packed in one go.

But, as they say, the best-laid plans go oft awry and just days ahead of the move William tripped on the stairs while carrying a large box, breaking several bones in his foot.

The accident delayed the family's move by eight crucial weeks and meant precious money that had been set aside for establishing themselves in Italy was now eaten up by unanticipated rent and storage bills. With her husband out of action and unable to work, Miranda took a temping job to lessen the financial blow, and William's collection of reclaimed building material, ranging from original terracotta tiles and wooden beams to fireplaces and window frames, was rapidly sold off. The family managed to keep themselves in pocket and finally, in July 2002, William drove their loaded truck to Tuscany, with Miranda, Annie and Isabella following by plane the next day.

Il Pero had cost the family a grand total of £277,000 (€413,785) and therefore had used up all the capital from the sale of their UK property. Miranda and William had a few savings with which to cover their living costs and get their massive project under way, but they also planned to mortgage the property and plough the proceeds straight back into it. Half of the main house was to be converted into two luxury apartments: Il Pastore, sleeping six people, with room for an additional two on pull-out beds; and Il Contadino, sleeping five people, with pull-out beds for an additional two. Il Pero's tower (La Torre) would become an open-plan mini-apartment with spectacular views; the perfect love nest for a romantic couple. A sizeable swimming pool needed to be installed and the rest of the grounds landscaped and planted with trees to provide shade. In due course one of the outbuildings, the old tobacco dryer, would be physically moved and converted into further guest accommodation. On top of this, William had to get one side of the main house, in which the family would be living, habitable and snug, *and* get electricity and running water installed. The Taxis' work was certainly cut out for them and their absolute priority was to redo the roof, which was leaking and causing further damage to the building's interior.

Before any of the work on the apartments could be started, it was necessary to get planning consent from the local authority and so their *geometra* (architect), Benigni, was briefed and he drew up plans, which were submitted in October. William and Miranda had been told that within twenty days of their submission they would be able to carry out vital work on the roof, but their dream was about to receive the biggest setback imaginable.

When their application was returned in mid-November the Taxis discovered, to their horror, that their plans for the restoration of Il Pero had been flatly rejected, and that was not where the bad news ended. Their new home was a building of architectural note and historical importance and, as such, it was protected by a system similar to the UK's Listing system, and it qualified for the highest rank. The upshot of this discovery was that the Taxis weren't able to touch a brick at Il Pero or begin the conversion. The Arezzo Commune planning authority was not going to allow them to make a living from luxury, converted apartments.

'We were absolutely shattered,' says William. 'Our local area is covered in Leopoldini houses which aren't listed, and plenty of other nearby buildings are medieval and considered to be of far more importance than a mere eighteenth-century farmhouse – that was practically considered a new-build here. It was a real shock to find out that it was listed. The discovery threatened the whole project and called into question whether we would be able to remain at Il Pero. We would have to rework the whole plan carefully, submit it again and pray that it was acceptable to the authorities. Of course, taking on the Italian bureaucracy is no mean feat and we knew it would be hugely time-consuming and would cost more precious money. Worst of all, it might get us nowhere. It was a big gamble, but we really wanted to make it work.'

Working closely with their *geometra*, the Taxis launched their second bid to cut through the Italian red tape and gain planning consent. New plans were submitted in December 2002 and once again the family was on tenterhooks awaiting the decision upon which their future was dependent.

'It was very hard to be passive,' explains Miranda. 'William visited the planning office every week to find out any news. It got to the point where he was on first-name terms with every one of the staff and several planning officers pretended to run away whenever they saw him enter the office! We also went to visit the Mayor of Arezzo to try and explain our plans to him. We knew he was a very influential man so we thought this might help our case.'

Unwilling to sit idly by and watch his beautiful house degenerate further with every rainfall, William started to work clandestinely. The half of the house that the family wanted to live in had a habitation permit and therefore William felt he could use the cover of this document to justify some work. This portion of Il Pero was in substantially better condition than the other half anyway, and because the work wasn't structural, William convinced himself that he wasn't breaking the law. He busied himself laying floors and clearing out rubbish, but as he was unable to hire builders until they received official permission, progress was achingly slow.

To add to the run of bad luck unjustly cursing the family, William suffered a serious accident while carrying out this secret work at Il Pero. He had borrowed a dumper truck from a friend so he could begin moving some of the rubble and earth that was beginning to fill their yard. Having been warned that the truck had faulty brakes, William was relying on the handbrake to halt the truck's progress. On this tragic occasion the handbrake wasn't enough to hold it and the truck hurtled into a ditch, flinging William onto some rusty corrugated iron. The result was devastating. Badly cut and losing a lot of blood, William's most serious injury was a gash to his neck that had severed his windpipe.

'I knew that I had had a bad accident but I didn't know how bad,' he recalls. 'I couldn't speak and I knew that a lot of blood was coming from my neck so I tied my T-shirt around it. I was working alone – Miranda was at the apartment in the village – so I had no choice but to get on my bike and cycle to her.

'By some dreadful coincidence, at about the time I had the accident, Miranda decided she would drive down and visit me on site. So when I arrived at our apartment there was no sign of her. I tried to call to someone for help but my voice was a small rasp and there was nobody around. By this time I was feeling pretty awful.'

When Miranda arrived back at the apartment, she found William covered in blood and listless. They headed straight for casualty.

'The health care was wonderful,' says William. 'Within two hours I was cleaned, X-rayed, scanned and stitched. I was told that I had been very lucky and that had the cut been an inch further in either direction I may have died. The staff were unsure as to whether I would recover my voice but they were pretty sure I was going to make it.'

Miranda was seriously shaken too. 'It was a terrible accident, made worse by the fact that it had happened in another country that I couldn't yet consider home,' she says. 'I didn't have the same level of Italian as William and, of course, he couldn't speak. This meant I couldn't communicate with the doctor very well, and as you can probably imagine, there were so many worried questions that I wanted to ask but couldn't. I went home from the hospital that night, put the girls to bed and just burst into tears; I felt so alone. It is at times like these that you need your family and friends around to support you. I even woke up in the middle of the night in a cold sweat, convinced that William had died in hospital.'

Despite the family's fears, William's miraculous survival was followed by a good recovery . . . probably made quicker by his experience of Italian hospitals.

'I can't find fault with the medical care I received, but aftercare seems to be non-existent in Italy. It is a very different system to the UK. When you are in hospital your family has to bring in everything for you, from cutlery to loo paper: none of it is provided. Similarly, nurses are there to administer medicine and bring you food, and that's where their duties end. Miranda had to come in to change my sheets – which were covered in blood – and wash my pyjamas. I couldn't eat for the first few days but when I was able to eat solids again I was fed this awful baby food. It tasted disgusting . . . Within five days I was desperate to leave hospital and finish my recuperation at home.'

And that is exactly what he did. Having obtained all the signatures that he needed in order to discharge himself, he was packed off home with a course of drugs. Still very weak, in a lot of pain and unable to speak, William could make no further progress with the house or the planning office for the next ten days. Gradually, though, with the help of Miranda and the girls, William regained his health, even recovering his voice. Of course, Isabella and Annie had been worried about their father but they had not really grasped the seriousness of his accident. Nonetheless, they were delighted when daddy was able to make jokes and laugh again, entertaining them at dinnertime by pretending spaghetti was spilling from the hole in his neck.

'It was a horrible time but at least we can laugh about it now,' says Miranda. 'What else can you do? The incident made our *No Going Back* programme very memorable; some friends of ours in England even jokingly accused us of pulling a desperate publicity stunt!'

Even with all that had happened in the meantime, the family were desperate for news of their renewed planning application. After an agonising four-month wait, William was summoned to the planning office with his *geometra* and finally given the news he had been waiting for – they had permission to transform Il Pero.

'It was a huge relief to be able to finally get started properly,' smiles William. 'We had been able to do bits and pieces on the side of the house that we were going to live in, under the dubious protection of the habitation licence, but now we had permission to go ahead with all guns blazing. We could now officially hire a full building team to crack on with the work. The delay had cost us dearly, so we decided that rather than do up the apartments and house gradually, we would plough all our resources into getting the apartments done so that we could start bringing in some desperately needed income.'

Of course, aside from the series of setbacks that steals the limelight of the Taxis' story, the family were settling into life in their village of Rigutino. William's language skills enabled them to meet and socialise with people easily, and Miranda's Italian came on in leaps and bounds too.

Il Pero was well known in the area and people were keen to meet the 'mad English people' who had decided to take on the wreck. Both William and Miranda admit that the kindly Orietta, a friend of William's mother and the lady from whom they had bought the house, was instrumental in pushing them into the community. She introduced them to everyone and took them along to every local *festa* so that people would start to recognise the family.

Isabella and Annie were young enough that the move was not a trauma for them; their parents knew that they would soon pick up the language and make more playmates. Even so, there is nothing quite as daunting as the first day of school. The Taxis had located a lovely little catholic church nursery (*azilo*), G. Meaci, in Rigutino, for children age two and a half to six. Isabella and Annie were both to attend.

'It was heartbreaking to see how terrified they were,' admits William, 'and very difficult to let them go: they really didn't want to. The school was run by nuns who looked very strange to them and, of course, all the other boys and girls were speaking Italian, which they didn't understand. It was all so alien to them.'

And if the girls were having a hard time at school, Miranda wasn't faring much better at the school gates.

'I took the girls to school and collected them every day,' she explains. 'I would stand at the gates with the other parents waiting for the bell to ring and they would all be chatting away. At this point my Italian wasn't very good, so no one really talked to me because after a few sentences it tended to get a bit awkward. But by the end of the school year I had learned enough to join in their conversations, and I like to think I'm a real part of the school-run crowd now.'

Once they had overcome their initial fear of the nuns now teaching them and learned a little of the language that surrounded them, the girls settled down. Within weeks it was clear that they had made some good friends and were interacting well with the other children. They weren't speaking very much but they seemed to be internalising a lot of the language and William and Miranda were delighted to overhear them testing each other's vocabulary.

With plans for Il Pero running seriously behind schedule, and no money coming in, Miranda went back to teaching. She started working a couple of mornings at G. Meaci school and also took a few students for private tuition, which brought in valuable euros. While William was busy with the house, Miranda also set about creating her very own kitchen garden, growing fruit, vegetables and herbs to supplement their groceries.

In April 2003 William was finally able to get his project going full swing. He went to the local builder's yard to ask for recommendations about local building teams who might be able to start work immediately. It was not long before Giorgio turned up at Il Pero in his BMW to assess the job.

'We agreed a price for the work and drew up a proper contract,' says William. 'There was even a clause that said we would receive financial compensation should the work overrun. I made it clear from the outset that I would expect the team to work very, very hard and that I would work with them most of the time. Giorgio was also informed that I was a builder myself so that I wouldn't be messed around.

'Despite all my misgivings, the team worked incredibly hard . . . and they still are, I really can't fault them. In fact the only near disaster we had with them was entirely our own fault.'

The massive renovation contract was to be funded by the Taxis taking a mortgage out on their property: they hoped to borrow in the region of £200,000. The bank had told William that this was not a problem, that the loan could be set up quickly and that they just had to wait for the agreement to come through in writing. This was enough for William and Miranda, who, after six months of stalling, were desperate to let their team loose on the house and see it start to come together as they had envisioned. The builders were paid their first instalment – the last of William and Miranda's savings – and battle commenced.

The first job listed on the building contract was the gate at the entrance of the property, which had to be built and have the electric meter fitted. This was achieved very easily. The next critical task was the roof, which needed to be water-proofed and insulated before winter. However, when the necessary materials hadn't arrived, the builders filled the time gap by laying reinforced concrete to support the original floor in what was to be the new apartments. This overlap in jobs meant that the next payment owed to the builders for the work that they had done was larger than the Taxis had originally calculated . . . they needed the mortgage payment fast.

The weeks ticked by and still no official word from the bank came through.

'It was an incredibly tense time,' says William. 'I chose not to be up front with the builders about the dire financial situation in case they walked out before finishing the roof. We were incredibly nervous but I just had to keep acting normal and pray that the money came through. They were desperately worrying times.'

The builders were due to be paid for their work in mid-August, just before going on their four-week holiday. The date loomed. In the nick of time, William received a call to let him know that the mortgage agreement had gone through and the funds were accessible to him. Almost overcome with relief, William drove to Rigutino to collect the builders' £60,000 just before they were due to go on holiday. To this day Giorgio and his team have no idea how close they came to missing out on their substantial pay cheque.

The conversion of half of Il Pero into apartments was a huge project and even with a team of hardworking builders progress was slow. Despite their tight budget and the obvious temptation to cut corners, Miranda and William have maintained a strong conviction that the restoration should be done lovingly and accurately. They have spent valuable time and money trawling through period salvage auctions to find replacement stone window ledges as well as recycling a lot of the original fabric of the house. In fact, according to their estimations, around 75 per cent of the roof tiles were salvaged, around 90 per cent of the floor timbers were salvaged and 50 per cent of the floor *cotto* (original eighteenth-century tiles).

The apartments, which were finally finished in April 2004, are beautiful, boasting fully equipped kitchens, Tuscan-style interiors and all modern conveniences, down to built-in hairdryers, English-style electrical sockets and adjustable bed springs.

The Taxis' own half of the house is the next priority for Miranda, though.

'We had decided to put all our money and effort into the apartments so we could start earning an income as soon as possible,' she says. 'But now I can't wait for William to sort out our house! Although it is habitable it has been a bit like camping for the last eighteen months. Washing-up is done in a bowl because there is no sink in the kitchen; an ancient boiler heats the water, so it is limited and temperamental, to say the least. We have had enormous fun and still love the property as much as, if not more than, when we first saw it, but some creature comforts would be really nice!'

The Taxis have had one of the roughest rides of all the families featured on *No Going Back*, and yet even when they overcome the hurdles of Italian red tape, planning bureaucracy, near-death experiences and dire financial worries, another problem rears its ugly head.

'The latest?' laughs Miranda. 'Well, we couldn't expect it to be plain sailing even with the apartments finished! Our most recent obstacle has been the mayor's plan to build a new international airport in the area. The big rectangle of land marked for the development starts around 200 metres from our house. It would be an absolute disaster, but fortunately everyone in the local area agrees. There is a huge campaign to stop the airport being built, and William has been on the committee since day one. It has really put us on the map as far as our neighbours go and has built an even bigger sense of community here . . . We even led a tractor procession to the mayor's office in protest. Fortunately he seems to have backed down for now, but the threat is still hovering.'

William and Miranda have also extended their business plans and, capitalising on all the knowledge they now have, are acting as house hunters for other Brits seeking a piece of beautiful property in Tuscany. They also run local lettings.

'It all came about by accident really,' says William. 'A few of our friends here have property they want to sell, so they asked if we might help them reach the UK market. Having navigated the Italian property market ourselves we know how difficult it can be, so we now offer the complete service to other people trying to make the same move – from finding property and making viewing appointments, to sorting out accommodation, translation, legal issues and even restorations. I think just about anything that can go wrong has gone wrong for us, so we're in a pretty good position to help others avoid the pitfalls!'

It is amazing that, after so many setbacks, Miranda and William have maintained their sense of humour and their firm belief that one day it would all work out. As testament to their hard work and determination, Il Pero now looks stunning and is ready for letting. The Taxis are a wonderful, warm family with a beautiful house in a lovely part of Italy, and after such a long wait, a visit is now highly recommended.

Il Pastore, Il Contadino and La Torre are all available for hire and prices start from as little as £80 per night. William and Miranda are happy to tailor your holiday specifically to your requirements, so if you fancy a painting holiday, or trying your hand at cooking or riding courses, just let them know.

You can contact them on tel. +39 05 75 979593 or visit their website at www.ilpero.com.

Top Tips

Miranda and William offer some advice:
- There is so much patronising advice being offered by people who have moved abroad, basically saying that you need to read thousands of books, do years of research and prepare yourself for every eventuality beforehand. To be honest, from our perspective there is absolutely no point. By all means find out the basics – things like how to buy a property and what paperwork you need to live and work in Italy – but every community is so different that the chances are what you have read will be irrelevant anyway. Arezzo has different ways of doing things from Pisa, for example.

Wherever you go, the learning curve will be enormous and the only way you will find out what to do is through trial and error. Every situation is different, as is every place you go – there is no definitive answer.

- Always be courteous and polite. The Italians are not, by and large, a courteous nationality. For example, if two cars meet on a narrow road here, the rule is that the bigger car has right of way and when you pass no one will acknowledge or thank you. They don't mean to be rude, it's just the culture here – everyone expects it and no one is offended. Having said that, if you do happen to be polite, people are really taken aback, but they also really like it . . . and the chances are they'll remember you. We have found a bit of courtesy has gone a really long way.

- Everything takes weeks. Don't EVER imagine that something will happen tomorrow, even if you are told it will. Just sit back and relax: no matter what you do or how much fuss you make, you will have to wait like everyone else. Don't get frustrated and try to fight the system – there is no point!

- Integration moves you along much more quickly. Don't become an outsider – and in a small, tight community this is easily done. When you live here, you will have to live like the Italians do, you have to go to local shops and chat.

- Nearly everything is negotiable in Italy, from food prices to fines. It's usually worth a try!

- This is one we got caught out on, so we want to make sure that you don't get caught out too – it can be a costly mistake, as we discovered. If you want to insure a car in Italy and you had a no-claims bonus in England, the Italian insurance company are legally obliged to accept it (providing they offer a no-claims bonus of some sort). The best company is probably Generale because they own a lot of English insurance companies. We didn't know our rights when we went to insure our Italian car and as a result it will take us twelve years to get our premium down to what we were paying in England!

Budget Sheet

How William and Miranda funded their move:
Although they set off on their quest with a large budget, William and Miranda found that it quickly drained away. The house they fell in love with cost far more than they had planned on spending and needed virtually complete renovation.

Financial tension was exacerbated by the bureaucratic hold-ups, which meant that Il Pero wasn't able to start earning money until much later than planned. Aware of just how far their money had to stretch, and knowing that their plight would be aired on national TV, William and Miranda took the clever step of approaching various companies and suppliers of the materials they needed to complete the conversion of the apartments and asked them to make donations. Kingspan Insulation (for whom Miranda had worked prior to leaving England) supplied the family with 900

Credit	Value (£s)
Sale of Herefordshire property	260,000
Savings/other assets	30,000
Mortgage on Il Pero	200,000
Total	**490,000**

square metres of insulation for their roof, while Armitage Shanks generously donated four pristine bathroom units of a quality suitable for the Taxis' luxury apartments. Wood is very expensive in Italy, so William and Miranda also approached Magnet, whom William had used as a supplier when undertaking building work in the UK. The company were hugely accommodating, sending out windows and window frames for the whole house and even throwing in a staircase for good measure.

This initiative saved William and Miranda thousands of pounds, shaving off a much-needed chunk from their outgoings. Now the apartments are up and running, it shouldn't be long before their huge financial, and emotional, investment starts paying for itself.

Debit	Value (£s)	Value (Euros)
Cost of buying Il Pero	280,000	418,246
Associated purchase costs	30,800	45,650
Services of Benigni	9,800	14,525
Work and labour	140,000	209,120
Decoration and equipment	20,000	29,874
Total	**480,600**	**717,415**

Practical Directory – Tuscany

Region

Tuscany is undoubtedly the most popular area of Italy for Brits. William and Miranda's *casa colonica* is actually situated in the village of Rigutino, in the reclaimed Val di Chiana and close to Tuscany's border with Umbria. Very rural and beautiful, the surrounding area is made up of rolling hills punctuated by cosy medieval villages and majestic eighteenth-century farmhouses. The Val di Chiana is known as one of the most fertile areas for agriculture in Italy and is covered in vineyards and olive trees. The nearby town of Arezzo (a fifteen-minute drive) caters for more practical needs with a range of supermarkets but, less conveniently, suffers from terrible rush-hour traffic. An important centre during Roman times, Arezzo boasts an amphitheatre as well as other stunning architecture spanning the centuries of its history. For more information visit http://www.provincia.arezzo.it or www.turismo.toscana.it.

Culture

As with most of Italy, typical Tuscan culture places a lot of importance on food. The family meal is virtually an institution, so if you would like to make friends with Tuscans, the best way to do it is to invite them over for a meal. Virtually all socialising is done face to face, over a meal, in the personal setting of someone's home. Family is another incredibly important facet of life for people in this area. If you invite a couple to your house, be prepared to cater for their children and any other friends or family they might have staying with them – it is taken for granted that the invitation will include all members of their household. Similarly, when you receive an invitation it will be open to everyone living with you.

William and Miranda love the fact that Italy is so child-friendly but they do miss having 'grown-up' time.

'Back in England we would have dinner parties with our friends and all sit around drinking and setting the world to rights,' explains William. 'That just isn't really done here. Don't get me wrong – we absolutely *adore* our kids, but we do miss being able to leave them with a babysitter once in a while and really let our hair down!'

Community is also a priority in Italy, particularly in villages like Rigutino. In order to integrate, make sure you go to local *festas* and get involved in events and committees as much as you can. You will find you are welcomed with open arms.

Another big association with Italy is, of course, fashion. Indeed, many inhabitants of the large towns and cities are very 'chic', looking elegant even to traipse around the supermarket. In the countryside, however, this is far less of an issue and rural residents usually have their clothing dictated to them by the extreme weather conditions.

Transport

If you are planning on moving somewhere similar to William and Miranda's area, you will need a car. There are bus services, but they can be sporadic. The trains are excellent and very good value for money but they often do not run to all the small villages. The Taxis' nearest train station is in Arezzo, fifteen minutes away by car. To check whether you can get to your destination by train see www.trenitalia.com (available in English).

Florence Airport is a forty-minute drive away but, as a flight destination, it can be expensive; try www.alitalia.com for any special deals. Ryanair have very cheap flights to Pisa (one and a half hours away) or Bologna (one and three-quarter hours away): see www.ryanair.com. British Airways sometimes do cheap deals too: see www.british-airways.com.

Jobs

Tuscany occupies an excellent geographical position and boasts an unemployment figure of just 5.2 per cent – well below the Italian average. The region hosts many strong and highly competitive industries including gold, fashion and furniture, as well as a lucrative export market for local produce such as agricultural and food products. These factors contribute to Tuscany's position as one of the wealthiest areas in Italy with a very high per capita income.

The service sector is probably the biggest employer and is constantly evolving; there is currently a need for professionals working in credit and insurance, businesspersons, construction carpenters, joiners and painters and nurses. There is also a deficiency throughout the IT sector and computer programmers are currently particularly sought after.

Recruitment

The system for finding work in Italy is very similar to that of most EU member states. For a comprehensive guide to living and working in Italy you can visit the Jobcentre Plus website (www.jobcentreplus.gov.uk) following links through 'Looking for a job'> 'Working or training in Europe' > 'Italy'. Jobcentre Plus is part of a network of Public Employment Services that belong to the EURES system (European Employment Services). EURES is a partnership of the European Economic Area (EEA) that exchanges information on vacancies and living and working conditions within the union. Throughout the EEA there are around 500 specially trained EURES advisors on hand to help you with queries; those in the UK can be contacted through your local Jobcentre Plus office. The website (http://www.europa.eu.int) contains listings with job vacancies from all over Italy. Both EURES and Jobcentre Plus can also offer you help and advice on CVs, applications and vacancy listings. For more information you can call Jobseeker Direct on +44 (0) 845 606 0234. The Italian equivalent to Jobcentre Plus is *Centro per l'impiego* and EU nationals are free to use the services on offer. Your nearest branch can be located in the telephone directory.

Private recruitment agencies operate throughout Italy but they must be authorised by the Ministry of Labour. Both temporary work agencies (*agenzie di lavoro temporaneo*) and permanent work agencies (*agenzie private di intemediazione*) can be found listed at www.minlavoro.it.

Newspapers carry job advertisements in their recruitment sections and are a valuable job-seeking resource. The main ones in Italy include *Corriere della Sera*, *La Repubblica* and *La Stampa*. Financial dailies include *Il Sole/24 Or* and *Italia Oggi*. In addition, there are English publications available for Italy that may prove useful. An example is the Yellow Pages, which contains listings for English-speaking professionals, businesses, organisations and services. It can be purchased from most bookshops or newsagents in the city concerned.

If you have a particular profession in mind and you want to find out more information on particular companies, it would be worth contacting the British Chamber of Commerce (*camera di commercio*) in Italy. Their contact details are as follows:

British Chamber of Commerce for Italy
Via Dante, 12
20121 Milano
Tel: +39 02 87 77 98/80 56 094
Fax: +39 02 86 46 1885
Email: bbci@britcham.com
Website: http://www.britchamitaly.com

House Prices

Being situated on the edge of sought-after Tuscany means that prices are lower than those that might be found in more central areas. Demand is quite high, however, as people who wish to buy a property in beautiful rural Italy are priced out of other areas. Near Arezzo you might be able to find a restored two-bedroom apartment in a village for between

£100,000 (€149,366) and £115,000 (€171,764). If you fancy something a little bigger and more challenging, £150,000 (€224,040) will probably buy you a large house (250 square metres) with a garden but in need of complete renovation. Should you prefer a property and challenge in the league of Il Pero, budget for at least a quarter of a million pounds sterling. Also bear in mind when considering a purchase of this kind that renovation costs can be crippling and many of the materials you want to salvage may be difficult to come across. William and Miranda have had to spend a small fortune, and an awful lot of time searching, in order to find original bricks, tiles and timbers to complete their project.

Tax

The Ministry of Economy and Finance administers the Italian taxation system through the *anagrafe tributaria* (tax registry department). Residents are issued with a *codice fiscale* (an individual fiscal code number), which serves to identify each taxpayer – it is actually necessary for all sorts of forms and it is advisable to carry it with you at all times. To obtain your *codice fiscale* you should contact your local tax office (*Ufficio Imposte Diretto*).

In Italy, taxes are generally divided into two groups: *tasse* (duty and public service taxes) and *imposte* (taxes regulated on the basis of income and capital gains). *Tasse* will include charges for services such as waste and refuse collection; they are not proportionally related to the service you receive but are actually a fixed compulsory tax. Students in secondary and higher education, for example, pay the *tasse scolastiche*.

The main *imposte* taxes are as follows:

- Income tax (*Imposta sul Reddito delle Persone Fisiche* or IRPEF). There are just two rates currently quoted for income tax. On earnings up to €100,000, it is applied at 23 per cent, and for anything over €100,000 it is applied at 33 per cent.

- Value Added Tax (*Imposta sul Valore Aggiunto* or IVA) is currently at 20 per cent

- Corporate Tax (*Imposta sulle Società*) is currently at 33 per cent

- The main local tax (*Imposta Comunale Immobili* or ICI) is calculated on the value of any property you might have. The rate varies from between 4 and 6 per cent.

The Italian tax system is very complicated and under reform. For this reason it might be a good idea to get some professional help. Many Italians employ the services of an accountant (*commercialista*) to manage their tax affairs.

For further information you can look at the Inland Revenue website which contains information on taxation and online versions of each of its forms: www.inlandrevenue.gov.uk.

Or you can contact:

Inland Revenue International Division (Double Taxation)
Victory House
30–34 Kingsway
London
WC2B 6ES
Tel: +44 (0) 20 7438 6622

Once in Italy, contact your local tax office, which will be listed in the telephone directory under *Uffici Finanziari*. For details of local taxes you will need to contact the town hall of the relevant *commune*.

Residency

Nationals of European Union member states may live in Italy without a residence permit for up to three months providing they hold a valid identity document or national passport. If you are from the EU and plan to stay more than three months you need to apply for a *Permesso di Soggiorno* (permission to stay), which can be obtained from the police headquarters (*questura*) of the relevant district. At the *questura* you will be given an appointment at the immigration office. The form you need to fill out to obtain your *Permesso di Soggiorno* corresponds to the standard one supplied by the Ministry of the Interior. It will ask you for the following:

- Your personal particulars

- Most of the information on your identity document (e.g. passport number)

- Date of entry into the district

- The reasons for your residence

- Your place of residence

- Any relative or dependant for whom you might also request residency

Your application must be accompanied by four identical

passport-size photos of yourself. You will need to take a valid identity document with you when you present your application, as well as either proof of employment (your contract) or proof of membership of the Italian National Health Service/the ownership of an insurance policy against sickness.

Be warned that the process is long and laborious with lots of legwork and waiting involved. From the police headquarters you will be referred to other local offices and your *Permesso di Soggiorno* may take some three months to be issued.

For more information, you can contact:

Ministry of the Interior (Ministero degli Interni)
Via del Viminale
Roma
Tel: 0039 06 46531

To ensure that you get the right paperwork before making your application, it might be wise to contact your nearest Italian Consulate office in the UK to check. Contact details for the office in London are as follows; there are regional offices as well.

Consulate General of Italy
38 Eaton Place
London SW1X
Tel: +44 (0) 20 7235 9371
Website: http://www.embitaly.org.uk

Another useful contact might be the Italian Embassy, although they do not deal with visa enquiries.

The Embassy of Italy
14 Three Kings Yard
London W1K 4EH
Tel: +44 (0) 20 7312 2200
Fax: +44 (0) 20 7312 2230

Education

Education in state schools is free though parents may be expected to pay for materials such as books. Compulsory education lasts nine years from ages six to fifteen. The Italian education system is currently undergoing a huge reform process, for which blueprints were still being drawn up at the time of writing. At present, state schooling exists as follows:

Nursery schools are optional for three- to five-year-olds.

Primary schooling lasts five years, beginning at the age of six. It is compulsory and the curriculum will incorporate a European language other than Italian as well as the use of computers.

Lower secondary schooling lasts three years and completes compulsory education. The orientation is varied and dependent on what the child wishes to go on to do. A second European language and Information Technology is mandatory. This phase concludes with a state examination, which, if passed, gives the child their lower secondary school diploma.

From here children can decide whether they wish to attend Upper Secondary school (grammar school) for five years where they will have the option to study such subjects as economics, linguistics, music, science and art and sit the state examination necessary for entry to University. Alternatively, they can choose to attend vocational or professional training to gain an occupational qualification. There are options for swapping between the two paths of study.

All children in Italy have the right to attend school until they are eighteen years of age. Higher education is divided into higher technical training – which leads to a specialisation certificate recognised throughout Italy – or University study – which typically involves a three-year degree course and the option for continued study.

Further information about education in Italy is available from your local office of *Provveditorato agli Studi* or by writing to the:

> Ministero della Pubblica Istruzione
> Viale Trastevere 76/A
> 00153 Roma
> Tel: (0039) 06/58491
> Website: http://www.istruzione.it

As with most of Europe, private schools are widespread in Italy. Most are Roman Catholic day schools. Any queries can be directed to the address above.

Similarly, international schools following an English curriculum and taught in English can be found in most major cities. For details contact:

> European Council for International Schools
> 21 Lavant Street
> Petersfield GU32 3EL
> Tel: +44 (0) 1730 268 244

Miranda has worked as a teacher both in England and in Italy, and says the following about Italian education: 'The school system is really hard on the kids because it is very oriented around literature and maths. Reading and writing are absolute priorities and activities such as music, sports and art aren't done in school. Isabella is six and now attends the local elementary school; she gets over an hour of homework every night. I personally think it is a little over the top and worry that she will be exhausted, but that is how it works in Italy, and she seems very happy which is the most important thing.'

Health

The Italian National Health Service or *Servizio Sanitario Nazionale* (SSN) ranks as one of the best health care systems in the world according to the World Health Organisation – it is also one of the least costly. Health care is free for every Italian resident providing you are paying social security contributions (so make sure you have your *Permesso di Soggiorno*). You will need to take your *Permesso* to the *Unita Sanitaria Locale* (USL) and obtain a national health number; the address of your local USL can be found in the supplement that comes with your phone directory. Self-employed or freelance workers should visit the *Istituto Nazionale della Previdenza Sociale* (INPS). There are regional offices throughout Italy but their address in Rome is:

INPS
Via Ciro il Grande 21
00144 Roma
Tel: (00 39) 06 59051
Website: http://www.inps.it

Only at this point can you register with a doctor (*medico convenzionato*). The choice of doctor is entirely yours and a list of them – as well as local health centres and hospitals – should be available from your local USL.

The SSN provides free hospital accommodation and sub-sidised medical treatment and prescriptions. Regions charge a fixed rate or 'ticket' for specific medical service; how much of this 'ticket' is subsidised will depend on your income. The elderly and people in low-income families will receive free care.

Of course the Taxis have experienced emergency medical care firsthand and were very impressed but there are aspects of the health system in Italy that William and Miranda feel leave a lot to be desired.

'My advice for parents is to bring out a huge supply of Calpol and Nurofen Junior,' says Miranda. 'Doctors here love antibiotics and prescribe them for coughs and colds, which I don't really agree with. The other big difference is that most medicines are not administered orally here. You will either be given suppositories or you are told to inject the medicine directly and are given syringes to take home. I really think this is traumatising for both the parent and the child. They don't seem to like doing things simply here, so unless I know the girls are really very ill, a little Calpol does the trick for me!'

Useful Contacts
Much of the information on these pages has come from EURES – the European Job Mobility Portal. For more infor-mation on any aspect of living and working abroad visit

their website at http://www.europa.eu.int. There is also a freephone helpline number: 00800 4080 4080.

A lot of information was also provided by Jobcentre Plus, who are part of the EURES network. For more information visit www.jobcentreplus.gov.uk or call Jobseekers Direct on +44 (0) 845 606 0234.

Property information was provided by property agents Casa Travella Ltd:

> Casa Travella
> 65 Birchwood Road
> Wilmington
> Kent
> DA2 7HF
> Tel: +44 (0) 1322 660 988
> Fax: +44 (0) 1322 667 206
> Website: http://www.casatravella.com

CHAPTER 9

From Hereford to Vrouhas

When Andie Cox and Marie Eversham met they shared the dream of doing something different with their lives; nine years later they got the chance.

On their first holiday together in Corfu in 1995, Andie and Marie saw a beach bar for sale. The property had accommodation above it and was in perfect condition; best of all was the price tag: just £80,000 (€119,470). Although the young couple were hardly in a position to contemplate the purchase – they had only been together for nine months and had no capital – they were stunned by the value for money and were very taken with the idea of running a business abroad. A seed was planted in both their minds . . . and this seed was to grow.

'It has never been "his" dream, it has never been "my" dream; it's something we both wanted to do,' explains

Marie. 'We have a very good relationship and we thought it would be great to work together. We also fancied doing something a bit different, to escape from the run-of-the-mill. The last thing we wanted was to stay in Hereford for the rest of our lives, just bringing home a salary. Neither of us is scared to try new things – we're the kind of people that just do them.'

It took nine years for that dream to come close to becoming reality, though. During that time the couple had wisely invested their money in property in their native Hereford and, two renovations later, were in a good position financially and mentally to make the move.

'There were other factors that pushed us to make the move at that particular time,' says Andie. 'Our son, Finley, was three years old and it was becoming apparent, as I think it does to any caring parent, that he was growing up really quickly. Because I spent around two hours commuting to work every day I could only snatch a few minutes with him before he went to bed. I worked in the automotive industry as a project manager and mentally my job was quite demanding. I would come home and just vegetate on the sofa, which I'm sure wasn't too much fun for Marie, who after a day of looking after Fin was probably looking forward to some grown-up conversation. It was the intention that when we moved abroad, we would spend more time together as a family.'

Let's face it, nine years is a long time to cherish a dream, so it is understandable that by the time Andie and Marie were in a position to act on that dream they had a very clear idea of exactly what they wanted.

'Above all, we wanted to live in a traditional village,' says

Andie. 'We didn't want to fit into this stereotype of 'Brits abroad', where they all go and socialise together, set up bingo nights and spend time discussing how wonderful Britain is. We wanted to live like local people.

'Also on the tick list was weather – we wanted a warm climate so that we could spend more time outside; we felt this was especially important for Fin. Finally, we wanted somewhere with letting potential.'

Armed with this wish list the couple scoured the Internet looking for suitable properties, until they found one in France. It was a beautiful old house, politely described by Andie as a 'former gentleman's residence', but with all the hallmarks of a mansion. Complete with twelve bedrooms, acres of land and an indoor swimming pool, it certainly had letting potential, but was in dire need of renovation. Having done a little investigation, it became clear that the French bureaucracy would not allow them planning permission to make the necessary changes on the property, so Andie and Marie reluctantly carried on their search.

Two of the hottest contenders in terms of location were Crete and Zante. The Coxes had spent many of their holidays either in Greece or on its islands and both were big fans of the culture, people and weather.

'We found a block of flats in Zante which we considered,' Andie recalls. 'But they were relatively new and had no character at all – they were just concrete blocks really. Somehow Crete always had the edge for us anyway; the island has a wonderful historical legacy. We reasoned that it was more of a tourist destination and we also thought the housing market was more developed, which would make it easier to buy and renovate – in retrospect I might well revise that opinion, but at the time that was what we thought! So we started hunting in earnest in Crete.'

The couple contacted various agents and arranged some viewings of promising properties. It was not long before they were boarding a plane bound for Heraklion airport to see for themselves what the Cretan property market had to offer. The jewel of their search was a 200-year-old house in the rustic village of Vrouhas. Vrouhas certainly fulfilled their criteria of a traditional village, replete with narrow winding streets, treasured lemon trees, higgledy-piggledy white-washed houses and, best of all, not another English face in sight.

The property itself was formerly a bakery. Situated in the heart of the village, it comprised several L-shaped buildings built around a yard, and to the back there was a 500-square-metre garden. In true Cretan style, the property had expanded over the years: the original structure was some two hundred years old but additions had been made at the turn of the century and yet more in the sixties. And because building styles had clearly not evolved too far in Vrouhas over the centuries, everything was built in the same way and of the same materials: stone and earth.

'It wasn't love at first sight,' admits Andie. 'I think I'm too practical for that. I could see that it needed an incredible amount of work. However, we could both see the potential and it had so much character. We decided that this was the one.'

Having sold their Hereford house for £125,000 and with equity from that of £95,000, the Coxes paid £55,000 (€82,136) for the old bakery, leaving around £40,000 (€59,720) for the substantial work.

It was an emotional goodbye to Hereford. Both Andie and Marie had grown up in the town and lived surrounded by friends and family. Their parents would miss them, and especially little Finley, enormously. Nevertheless, in July 2003, the Coxes set off.

Their arrival in Crete was not quite as they had hoped. The container that held all of their belongings, including Andie's tools, Finley's toys and even pre-purchased UK toilets and plumbing, was delayed by two weeks. The original plan was to stay in a hotel for a fortnight while they gradually unpacked their possessions and secured with doors and a waterproof tarpaulin the room of the bakery they were to live in temporarily. Without tools, none of this could happen, so the family accepted that they would have to rent an apartment for a while and concentrated on another important task . . . installing running water.

The bakery had no water supply and, as such, was completely uninhabitable for the young family. Andie and Marie had devoted considerable time and effort trying to set the wheels in motion via their solicitor while they were still in England, but to no avail. Now they were 'on the ground' in Crete, they hoped to get things moving more quickly. To their amazement, even visiting the solicitor's office every day failed to produce results – the Coxes were experiencing their first taste of the laissez-faire attitude that was to push them almost to breaking point over the coming months.

'The most frustrating thing is that you are told it will only take a day,' grins Marie. 'You end up wasting so much time. Whenever you go in and try to confront someone about it, they just pass the buck. Customer service is absolutely non-existent here and trying to figure out exactly what is the hold-up is impossible. You just have to accept that everything will take for ever.'

Three weeks after their arrival in Crete (and seven weeks after their initial request) the Coxes' bakery received a water supply, albeit to an outside tap. Delighted, the family were able to move into the derelict wreck they were learning to call home. Andie wasted no time getting the work under way. The amount they had to get through was staggering and they were determined to be finished and ready for business by April 2004 (eight months later) in order to capitalise on their first summer season.

Not even the structure was sound. All the roofs needed replacing and all the stone walls needed to have the earth that had been used as mortar chiselled out and replaced with cement. Interior walls needed to be moved and knocked through, windows needed to be put in, the earth floors needed concreting and the whole place needed to be plastered and decorated. The gardens needed taming and landscaping, they wanted to have a pool installed, and the whole place needed new electrical wiring. Probably most important of all, they needed to fit flushing, indoor toilets.

'The living conditions were very difficult for that first winter,' comments Andie. 'Coming from a civilised country you really take for granted luxuries such as having an indoor toilet. Having to go outside is fine in the summer, but the sun doesn't always shine in Crete. When the hailstones are crashing down in the middle of the night and your little boy needs the loo and can't wait, it is a different story. We didn't have an indoor toilet for the first seven months that we lived here.

'People live very simply here. Most people in Vrouhas have a single-room house with an outside toilet; that is just the way it has always been. The property we have is by no means large – we have converted it into three apartments, but in Cretan terms it was the equivalent of eight or nine houses.'

'Things got even worse when the structural work got under way,' adds Marie. 'Then we were living on a building site. At that point not even the locals could believe our living conditions, but you just get used to it. Fin was wonderful. Obviously it's not ideal for a three-year-old to live surrounded by hazards, but he had a great time. If there was a big pile of dirt dumped in the yard, then he viewed it simply as something to run up!'

Not long after their arrival in Crete, Finley began attending nursery. As he was quite a timid child, and so young, Andie and Marie were nervous about sending him to a Greek nursery, yet were keen for him to integrate and learn the language. A happy medium was quickly found.

'Fin goes to a private Greek nursery a few kilometres away,' explains Marie. 'Here he is taught in Greek and is surrounded by local children but the teachers can speak English too. This means that if he gets very confused, or just desperate for the toilet, he will be understood in English, which was important for our peace of mind. Having said that, his Greek is coming on well: he has picked up the language very quickly. We've only been here a year and yet he will chat away to his Mr Men using Greek words. It's almost like it's not another language to him – he feels like he is just learning new words. The teachers are delighted with him; apparently he joins in with all the Greek songs they sing and the Greek games they play.'

With Finley at nursery for a few hours a day, Marie had some time to help her husband with the renovation . . . and he needed all the help he could get. Andie had hired an architect to plan and supervise the project. Not being a Greek-speaker himself, Andie had hoped that the architect would liaise with their building team, help source materials and generally make the whole project easier, but it quite soon became apparent that Andie had been too optimistic.

The architect was very rarely on hand, or even on site, to help with even the most basic tasks. Andie rapidly became incredibly frustrated that whenever a small problem cropped up that he hoped to sort out before it became a bigger problem, the architect was unavailable. Worst of all were the times that Andie's builders, who were being paid by the hour, stood around doing nothing because the architect had failed to deliver the necessary materials at the correct times. Although the architect continued to handle the Coxes' official renovation permit, by the beginning of 2004 he was effectively off the job in terms of supervising the actual project.

'It was a big blow that our architect let us down,' says Andie. 'I found it very difficult because we didn't really speak any Greek when we first moved here and suddenly I had to liaise with all the builders and contractors myself. It was a bit of a crash language course. I can now make myself understood in Greek building terms and if all else fails there is always the international language of gestures. I can't discuss politics or culture in Greek but I can tell you where I want the wall, how high I want it to be and what it should be made of!'

The building team themselves proved a source of frustration too. Lacking the sense of urgency felt so keenly by Andie and Marie who were desperate to meet their May deadline, the men took regular and lengthy breaks and Andie felt the need to supervise them at all times.

'There have been so many delays and hold-ups,' sighs Marie. 'Although we opened on time we could have been finished a lot earlier and with a lot less hassle. Andie has been working throughout and I have helped wherever I can, so even when the builders weren't doing anything there was some progress being made.'

To add further complications to the Coxes' Cretan adventure, shortly after they moved out to Crete Marie fell pregnant. Though delighted with the news and thoroughly looking forward to the arrival of Fin's new playmate, Marie and Andie did find the experience difficult. In both of the previous renovations they had carried out the couple had been equal partners, sharing the workload and the stress. With the best will in the world, Marie was going to have to take a back seat on this one, though she proudly admits that she was chiselling earth out of the stone walls eight months into the pregnancy.

'It was quite a frightening experience,' she explains frankly. 'The system was just so different to that in England. There were no fixed appointments or check-ups; I just had to turn up at the hospital and wait to be seen. Of course my doctor spoke English, but there are limitations. I really didn't feel like I could ask all the questions I wanted to, so it was quite stressful. One particular quirk that I found really odd was that as soon as my due date had passed, the gynaecologist wanted to induce the birth. I found it really ironic after all the problems we had had: it seems that childbirth is about the only thing they are worried about getting done on time!'

Despite her worries, on 19 February Marie gave birth to a bouncing baby boy, Cawley.

The couple both agree that one of the main things that has made their whole experience in Crete more bearable is the local people. Despite the massive language and culture barrier, Andie and Marie, and especially Fin, have been welcomed with open arms into the little close-knit community.

'Most of the people in the village are fairly elderly,' says Marie, 'and they all think Fin is wonderful. I think it has a lot to do with the fact that he is fair; there aren't many children in the village but those that do live here are typically dark-haired. Although Andie and I would have experienced no problem on our own, I think Fin has helped to integrate us really quickly. It is such a child-friendly culture over here; he is an instant talking point and people love to stop and make a fuss of him. It's so nice that people don't worry about being affectionate here: both men and women will stop to talk to him and pick him up and pet his hair. The amount of chocolate and sweets he gets bought is ridiculous!

'Fin is very happy here, though it was a bit strange for him at first. Before he understood any of the language he would try and play with the village children and be very confused about why they didn't answer any of his questions, or talk to him when he gave them something. Now that he knows enough Greek, things are much easier.'

'The people here are wonderful,' confirms Andie. 'It really is like stepping back in time. The people of Vrouhas live so simply and clearly don't have much money but they don't seem to ponder on it at all. The old woman who lives next door owns a donkey and some goats, she makes her own cheese, bakes her own bread and even distills her own *raki*, which is lethal! Another one of our neighbours always brings us home-baked cakes and some eggs. It is amazing how generous they are, given how little they have. When Marie and Fin went back to England for a month to visit family and friends, the village people cooked me a meal every day; they really rallied round.

'I think us moving here was stranger for them in many ways. They know that the standard of living in the UK is very high so they can't understand why we have come to live here.'

With the Coxes' project – Vrouhas Vines – now complete, the family can finally relax a little and enjoy some of the creature comforts that they have missed for so long.

'Looking back, it is hard to imagine how we lived while the building was going on,' laughs Marie. 'Now we are the poshest people in town, with flushing toilets and a swimming pool! Of course we won't forget the kindness that the people here have shown us. It is nice to be able to return some favours now and invite them round for a meal . . . They can even have a dip in the pool if they fancy it!'

Vrouhas Vines offers two stone cottages as guest accommodation, sleeping between four and six people each. Board is on a bed-and-breakfast basis and prices include bike hire, car hire, airport collection and a welcome basket. Facilities at Vrouhas Vines include a swimming pool, plunge pool and

children's play area. For more information call 0030 2841
0425 79 or visit http://www.traditionalgreekholidays.com.
Email mail@traditionalgreekholidays.com.

Top Tips

*Andie and Marie offer some advice based on their
experiences:*

- If you move to a small, traditional village like Vrouhas,
  you must be prepared for a massive change in lifestyle.
  Stepping back in time is very charming, but can you
  really live without those creature comforts? No one
  here speaks English, so we have had to learn very fast.
  There is also no social life to speak of, we don't go out
  and most of the people we live near are pretty elderly.
  We have also had huge difficulty getting a decent
  electricity supply. People's needs here are very small but
  we want a washing machine and sufficient electricity to
  power the three houses, which it has been a struggle to
  get.

- You have to accept that your plan probably won't run
  to budget AND to time, it'll be one or the other – you
  choose.

- You need to be very well organised. Pre-plan every last
  detail at least five years ahead and you might be
  finished on time! More realistically, don't get too hung
  up on deadlines and timescales: it won't happen as you
  want it to – a project out here is far more difficult to
  manage than anything in the UK would be. You have to

get used to the system here because it has been this way for ever and they aren't going to change it for you. The attitude to customer service here is very different from the UK too. You can never just speak to the manager if you don't like the way you are being treated – the chances are that he/she won't care! The customer is always wrong here and even if you shout you won't be heard. You just have to relax, let it go and accept that things happen in their own sweet time.

- If you are planning on conducting building work in a little village like Vrouhas, do consider important factors such as access. We had real problems getting large-scale machinery on site through the narrow streets. Fortunately our neighbours were very obliging, knocking down a wall and cutting off the branches of a prize lemon tree so that we could get our mixer in.

Budget Sheet

How Andie and Marie funded their move:
Financially, things were very tight for Andie and Marie. Good planning was crucial to their being able to pull off the project. Having had previous experience of renovations, the couple could price the work realistically and did a lot of their homework before leaving the UK. Although the work did go over budget it was by a marginal, and affordable, amount and, more importantly, the Cox family were able to welcome their first guests on time and start bringing in much-needed income.

Credit	Value (£s)
Sale of Hereford house	125,000
Total	**125,000**

Practical Directory – Crete

Region

Crete is Greece's largest island, with a population of around 600,000. It is becoming an increasingly popular destination for holiday makers, and now receives around a quarter of all of Greece's visitors. For this reason parts of the north have become quite overrun by tourism, though there are still plenty of opportunities to escape it.

The Coxes bought their property in the small, traditional village of Vrouhas on the eastern section of the island in the province of Lassithi. There are several villages in this area that have fallen victim to tourists, but if you travel further away from the main roads you will discover quaint yet bustling communities, such as that found at Vrouhas. In fact, some of the province is almost entirely untouched. Soon after you leave the tourist centre of Agios Nikolaos – a tasteful

Debit	Value (£s)	Value (Euros)
Mortgage to be paid off on Hereford property	30,000	44,790
Cost of Crete property	47,000	72,000
Associated purchase costs	6,000	10,000
Cost of shipping belongings	4,000	5,971
Cost of renovation	47,000	70,000
Total	*134,000*	*202,761*

resort town – the majestic and rocky coastline descends into sparkling, clean sea punctuated regularly by secluded, sandy coves. Despite the airport being close by, planes are not allowed to cross Crete and so the feeling of stepping back in time is preserved.

For further tourist information visit http://www.crete-travel.com or contact:

Greek National Tourism Organisation
4 Conduit Street
London
W1S 2DJ
Tel: (Enquiries & Information) 020 7495 9300
Fax: 020 7287 1369
Email: info@gnto.co.uk
Website: http://www.gnto.gr

Culture

Like much of Greece, there is a strong sense of family in Crete and socialising revolves primarily around events such as weddings, birthdays and name days. Relaxation time – of which there is plenty – is usually spent in the local *kafenion* (café) eating enormous leisurely meals or simply watching the world go by over a glass or two of *raki*.

Food is an incredibly important aspect of life on Crete. The local diet revolves around the vast amount of organic fruit and vegetables grown on the island, and it is thought to be responsible for the fact that Cretans have one of the longest average lifespans in Europe. Traditional Cretan cuisine doesn't include much meat but has perfected delicious *meze* dishes such as *dolmades* (stuffed vine leaves), olives and goat's cheese. *Tavernas* will often serve food made to local, and most probably ancient, family recipes which will combine lots of different herbs and a great deal of ingenuity and versatility – it is reckoned that there are over forty ways to cook snails on this island.

A delightfully hospitable and nosy people, it is unusual for the village not to know your business, but you will rarely leave a Cretan house without receiving some small gift or token.

Transport

The closest airport to Andie and Marie is the international one at the island's capital – Heraklion. For excellent-value flights from most UK destinations (Gatwick, Heathrow, East Midlands, Manchester, Glasgow and Belfast) try Excel Airways (http://www.excelairways.com). Monarch (http://www.monarch-airlines.com), Olympic (http://www.olympic-airways.gr) or

British Airways (http://www.british-airways.com) might also be worth a look for special offers. Excel and Olympic also fly to Chania, on the western side of Crete.

Once in Crete, buses are the main form of public transport, running a frequent service along the main highways and to the villages. There is also an excellent school bus service in Crete.

People often use bikes to get around in Crete, but be warned that strong leg muscles are required to tackle the often mountainous terrain. There is also an extensive ferry network connecting mainland Greece and the islands.

Jobs

In 2001 Crete had one of the lowest unemployment rates in Greece, just 6.7 per cent. Since then the Greek economy has undergone massive restructuring, making the employment climate difficult to monitor, though there is little evidence to suggest that unemployment levels will have changed significantly. Most people who really want to work in Crete are unlikely to have difficulty in finding employment, particularly in tourist areas during the tourist season. Language will always be a problem for most trades and industries, with the possible exception of construction, and for many jobs you will need to speak good Greek.

Recruitment

The system for finding work in Crete is very similar to that of most EU member states. For a comprehensive guide to living and working in Crete you can visit the Jobcentre Plus website (www.jobcentreplus.gov.uk) following links through

'Looking for a job'> 'Working or training in Europe' > 'Greece'. Jobcentre Plus is part of a network of Public Employment Services that belong to the EURES system (European Employment Services). EURES is a partnership of the European Economic Area (EEA) countries that exchanges information on vacancies and living and working conditions within the union. Throughout the EEA there are around 500 specially trained EURES advisors on hand to help you with queries; those in the UK can be contacted through your local Jobcentre Plus office. The website (http://www.europa.eu.int) contains listings with job vacancies from all over Greece. Both EURES and Jobcentre Plus can also offer you help and advice on CVs, applications and vacancy listings. For more information you can call Jobseeker Direct on +44 (0) 845 606 0234.

Organismos Apasholisseos Ergatikou Dynamikou (OAED) is an office of the Manpower Employment Organisation and serves as the equivalent of the Jobcentre throughout Greece. Its services are free for EEA nationals and your local branch can be located in the telephone directory *(tilephonikos odigos)*. If you require any information which cannot be provided by the OAED, you can contact the EURES section at the OAED headquarters:

OAED
EURES (SEDOC)
Ethnikis Antistasis 8
16610 A. Kalamaki
Tel: +30 21 994 2466/21 0998 9000
Email: ird1@oaed.gr
Website: http://www.oaed.gr/mainenglish

Private employment agencies are forbidden by law in Greece. Those that are allowed to operate are called *Grafia Evrésseos Ergassías* and can be found in the equivalent to the Yellow Pages (*Chryssos Odigos*).

Although regional and local newspapers may carry recruitment listings within them, probably the most important medium for job hunters is word of mouth – keep your ears open and your eyes peeled for opportunities.

Another good port of call would be the Chambers of Commerce both here in the UK and in Greece. Try:

British Hellenic Chamber of Commerce
Vas Sofias Avenue 25
10674 Athens
Tel: +30 210 721 0361
Fax: +30 210 721 2119
Website: http://www.bhcc.gr

The Chamber of Commerce of Heraklion
9 Koronaiou Street
71202
Heraklion
Tel: +30 2810 229 013
Website: http://www.ebeh.gr

House Prices
The demand for second homes in Crete is growing and keeping the market very buoyant. There is a huge spectrum of properties available, starting from around the price of an executive car here in the UK – £15,000 (€22,390) will buy

you a stone village house in need of complete renovation, for example. Move up to £40,000 (€59,700) and you can take out the hassle of doing the renovation yourself. New-build properties clock in at around £65,000 (€97,000), while luxury villas with private pools might command £150,000 (€223,870). With property prices sitting comfortably lower than those found in most Mediterranean countries, you can definitely bag yourself a bargain in Crete, but do bear in mind that while prices will rise they are unlikely to experience the exponential growth witnessed in some European markets.

If you are thinking of buying for investment, a carefully chosen property can earn you a reasonable rental income as the weather allows a long tourist season.

Tax

To gain full information about what national and local taxes you will be subject to when living in Crete, it is best to visit your local tax office (*efories*). General information can also be obtained from the Ministry of Finance (*Ypourgio Ikonomikon*) at the address below:

Ypourgio Ikonomikon
Tmima Diethnon Scheseon
Sina Street 2-4
101 84 Athens
Tel: +30 01 360 4825

Income tax or *Foros Issodimatos* is deducted at source on a monthly basis; adjustments are made annually. For more information contact:

Inland Revenue International Division (Double
Taxation)
Victory House
30–34 Kingsway
London
WC2B 6ES
Tel: +44 (0) 20 7438 6622

The Inland Revenue website contains information on taxation and online versions of each of its forms: http://www.inlandrevenue.gov.uk

Other taxes

Value added tax (VAT) is payable and called *Foros Prostithemenis Axias* (FPA). There may also be duties to pay when importing certain items (including household goods) into Greece. For further details contact the Customs and Excise office in the UK. Their national advice line is 0845 010 9000, or you can look at their website http://www.hmce.gov.uk. Once in Greece, you will need to contact the local customs authority or *teleonia*.

Local taxes

Owners of properties are subject to a very small Public Tax which is incorporated into the electricity bill and is payable every second month.

Property taxes

The passing of a new law recently means that owners of real estate property whose 'assessed value' or 'objective value' exceeds €175,000 (£120,000), or €350,000 (£240,000) for a couple, are subject to property taxes. For example, a real estate property owned by one person with an 'objective value' estimated at €322,800 (£221,000) would be subject to an annual tax of about €440 (about £300).

Residency

If you plan to stay in Greece for less than three months either working or looking for work, all you need to do is register with your local police station within eight days of arrival. If you intend to stay longer you will need to obtain a residence permit – again from your local police station *(Astynomia)*. It is always wise to contact the UK-based Greek consulate before leaving for Greece to get up-to-the-minute information on what documents and procedures are required. Their address is:

> Consulate General of Greece
> 1a Holland Park,
> London
> W11 3TP
> Tel: +44 (0) 20 7221 6467
> Email: consulategeneral@greekembassy.org.uk

Education

State education is free and compulsory for all children from the age of five or six to fifteen. Children can start their schooling at a younger age in a nursery *(nypiagogeia)*, but this stage is optional.

Primary schooling lasts for six years, at the end of which children receive a certificate of studies which is needed for their enrolment into secondary school at age twelve.

Secondary school is divided into two cycles: the first three years are spent in *gymnasium*, after which children receive a certificate of completion. The next three years can be spent in *lyceums*. *Lyceum* are divided into three main types: general, classical and technical/professional. In Greece, children start learning English in their fourth grade of primary school. For further information on the Greek education system, contact:

> Greek Embassy
> Education Office
> 1a Holland Park
> London W11 3TP
> Tel: 00 44 (0) 20 7 221 5977
> Website: http://www.greekembassy.org.uk

or the Greek Ministry of Education and Religion (*Ypourgio Pedias & Thriskermaton*):

> Ypourgio Pedias & Politismou
> Metropoleos Street 15
> 10 185 Athens
> Tel: (00 30) 01 323 0461

Information on private and international schooling can also be obtained from the above addresses.

Health
Idrima Kinonikon Asfalisseon (IKA) runs the Greek national health system. Once you start paying social security contributions, you can visit your local IKA office and obtain an

iatrico vivliario (medical booklet), which should be taken with you on all visits to the doctor or hospital. The IKA can also provide you with a list of local doctors working under the national health system. If you are in Greece, then contact any IKA office or the International Relations Office (*Tmima Diethnon Scheseon*) at the following address:

> IKA
> Tmima Diethnon Scheseon
> Kifissias Avenue 178
> 152 31 Athens
> Tel: (00 30) 01 647 1140

Though treatment, doctor's appointments and hospital care are free, the standard is quite rudimentary due to chronic underfunding. State hospitals (*yenikó nosokomío)* are basic and the cost of nursing is not covered by the health care system. For this reason, private health care – though expensive – is quite widespread. Things are improving, though, and EU criteria are ensuring that reforms are being pushed through and investment in the public sector is increasing.

For minor complaints you can always pay a visit to the *farmakio* (pharmacist). In Greece they are highly trained and can dispense medicine that elsewhere might only be available from a doctor. In larger towns and resorts you will usually be able to find one who speaks English.

Useful Contacts

A lot of information on these pages was provided by Jobcentre Plus, who are part of the EURES network. For more information visit http://www.jobcentreplus.gov.uk or call Jobseekers Direct on +44 (0) 845 606 0234.

Additional information was supplied by property agents Crete Property Consultants (Andie and Marie used them to buy their property in Greece):

Oonagh and Cassie Karanjia
Crete Property Consultants
78 Gascony Avenue
London NW6 4NE
Tel: *(during office hours)* 020 7328 1829
Fax: 020 7328 8209
Email: oonaghk@btinternet.com
Website: http://www.creteproperty.co.uk

CHAPTER 10

From London to Landes

Benn Coley and Amy Jenkins were high-flying city executives until they were presented with an opportunity they couldn't pass up.

Benn Coley's job was stressful and demanding. As a qualified chartered accountant during the dot-com boom, he had landed himself the position of financial director in a dot-com advertising agency. As the economy took its grim toll on the blossoming industry, however, Benn found himself responsible for a lot more than he had originally bargained for.

'The company wasn't doing well,' he explains. 'We were constantly striving to build it back up to what it had once been. I was trying to find enough money to pay people at the end of the month. The pressure was enormous because I was constantly firefighting. I used to take work and stress home with me because I just couldn't walk away.'

His fiancée Amy, a self-employed stenographer at the high courts, also fancied a career change. Although her work was financially rewarding, it was intense and, after twelve long years in the profession, she was sick to death of it.

'I was a bit panicked, I suppose,' she recalls. 'Ideally I wanted to retire but that isn't really an option when you're thirty! I needed a new direction that I didn't have to retrain for and was actually contemplating something along the lines of opening a bar.'

Installed in a chic apartment in Wimbledon, the couple lived London life to the full, enjoying a large circle of friends and plenty of nights out on the town.

'Socially, things were hectic too,' Benn grins. 'We were out a couple of nights a week and weekends were just mad. Although I loved socialising, I was beginning to get tired of the routine. Waking up on Saturday with a hangover, recovering just in time to do it all again on Saturday night and then feeling shattered back at work on Monday. I was growing out of it, I guess. I wondered if I was ever going to do the things I wanted to do.'

Amy, a city girl through and through, is happy to admit that her life outside of work revolved around shopping.

'I was famous for my outfits and my shoes,' she laughs. 'I was getting tired of it, though; I wanted to relax – having to keep up an image can be hard work. The thing that was driving me really mad, though, was living a life dominated by my diary. I hated knowing that I didn't have a free day for the next three months; I hated trying to make an arrangement to go out and get drunk with my girly friends but between all three diaries the only time we could manage would be some time next year. There just seemed to be no time for anything.'

While both tiring of their hectic London life and craving career changes, the couple lacked the trigger that they needed to make a life change. The circumstance that created this trigger came about soon enough, though, and it came in the form of an inheritance. Benn's mother had passed away a couple of years earlier and he finally received his share of her estate. Wanting to invest the money wisely, Benn had decided that he would use the money as a deposit on a holiday house.

'My immediate thought was to buy a property in Cornwall,' he admits. 'I love surfing, though I don't get to go often, and I thought a house down there would be perfect for my friends and me whenever we got the chance. I even got as far as thinking I could rent it out at other times of the year.'

Amy, however, had other ideas.

'I HATE Cornwall,' she laughs. 'Having a holiday home there really is my idea of hell. Bank holiday rolls around and you spend fifteen hours sitting in traffic to get there. Once you arrive you get to sit on a cold, windy beach with sand blowing in your face. Two days later you have to sit in traffic for fifteen hours to get home again. That's not fun!'

Fortunately, it seems that Benn did not have his heart set on Cornwall, and when Amy suggested that he buy a holiday home overseas instead, he was taken with the idea.

It didn't take long for the couple to come up with Biarritz as a location that catered for their very different tastes. The surfing on the local beaches is renowned as among the best in Europe, while the glamour – and shopping facilities – of the city itself were more than enough for Amy. Without further hesitation, Benn and Amy contacted an agent and went to visit some properties.

'The woman that we dealt with at the agency was lovely,'

says Benn, 'but something went wrong between me giving her what I thought was a clear, succinct brief and her passing it on to the representative in Biarritz. When we arrived and met with him, he didn't have any two-bedroom apartments in the city – he specialised in châteaux. He was quite shocked by our budget of £100,000 (€149,240) too; it seems that doesn't get you far in this part of the world. He literally had to dust off a book he had stored in the corner of his office containing properties in that price range.'

The agent had just three properties close to Benn and Amy's budget. They agreed to see two of them out of curiosity; their hunt for a Biarritz crash pad would have to wait until their next trip. Both houses were a half-hour drive from Biarritz, one of which was in a small town called Pouillon. The first was little more than a shed and was dismissed out of hand by the couple, but the second caught their eye.

'I was in shopping mode,' Amy giggles. 'You know, off to France to buy a house . . . ooooh, I quite like that one. It was a very impressive property and quite a mad design, two factors that appealed enormously to me. Of course, it wasn't what we were looking for at all, we had only gone to view it to make the best of a bad job because there was nothing else to see, but I fell in love with it.'

Benn was struggling to be more realistic. 'It was too big, and at £200,000 was far more than we had planned to spend, but I can't deny that it had something. Trying to be practical, the only thing that held my interest in it was the fact that the property was split in two, so there was some potential for letting.'

In comparison to their original brief, the house was enormous. There were eight bedrooms, two living rooms, two kitchens and a large basement. What would they do with all that space? the couple tried to reason. As a holiday home to be visited only a couple of times a year, the house was wildly extravagant, so they returned to the UK empty-handed.

Within a matter of days, the agent from Biarritz was on the phone wanting to know what they had thought. Ben tactfully explained that, while they really liked the property, it was too big, too expensive, and altogether not what they had in mind. The agent had the solution to at least one of these doubts.

'He told us that because the property had been on the market for some time and the owners had had two sales fall through on them, they were likely to accept a lower offer,' says Benn. 'He suggested offering £150,000. It seemed so ludicrous for such a big property that we agreed. We were astounded when he came back and told us that for £160,000 we could have it.'

Although the price tag was over what they had planned to spend, it was not beyond the realms of possibility, and, knowing that they had bagged themselves a real bargain – even if they had no idea what to do with it – the couple decided to buy the property.

February 2002 brought with it another trip to France to sign the *compromis de vente,* and this visit set both Benn and Amy's imaginations on fire. They loved the lifestyle, they loved the culture, they loved the location and they loved the beaches. How were they ever going to drag themselves back to London after a holiday in such a beautiful place?

By this time they had done some research and, upon discovering that many French families rent rather than buy property, the couple had decided that the larger part of the house could be rented out on an annual basis while they would keep the smaller part for their own private use. It all seemed very simple, but somehow unsatisfactory.

'One Friday night we went out for a curry and a few bottles of wine and got talking about the house,' Amy smiles. 'We were very drunk but we both admitted that we were desperate to find a way to live out there permanently because we loved it so much. I was delighted because I really didn't think Benn had been moved by France in the same way I had, but it turns out we had been having pretty much the same thoughts all along. I love playing the hostess and catering – I was used to having big dinner parties – so I had been thinking that we could run holidays.'

Benn was keen to add his ideas to the melting pot too. As a lover of the outdoor life, and all things active, he saw himself adding adventure to the holidays, offering guests anything from rafting and surfing, to skiing and biking. On the back of a serviette French Fusion holidays was born.

Waking up the next morning with hangovers, the couple came back down to earth with a bump. As they recalled the previous night's conversation, they reasoned that it was probably just a dream. How could they ever undertake something like that and give up all they had in London? But the thoughts never seemed to go away and they became a constant topic of discussion. They were tormenting themselves and both of them eventually agreed there was nothing for it but to give it a shot.

'We had got to this junction in our lives where we wanted a change,' says Benn. 'We were both tired of our lives and professions and it seemed like an ideal time to just go for it. We didn't have to consider kids, and we were young enough that if it all fell through we could come back to London to pick up the threads of our previous lives. There was just no reason not to do it.'

Used to the vagaries of the UK property market, Benn and Amy weren't going to count any chickens until they had completed on the house. Their plans to do this were put on hold for a further couple of months for reasons beyond their control. Some kids who had been using the empty property as a playhouse had accidentally set the smaller house on fire, destroying the roof. The couple waited until the rebuild was complete before signing the final *acte de vente*. This was duly accomplished in May and, to their delight, Benn and Amy realised that they had done rather well out of the potentially catastrophic fire. The vendor's insurance had paid for a new roof and a new upstairs floor in the smaller house. Despite the fact that they had no intention of moving to France for at least a further six months, Benn and Amy wasted no time in laying the foundations of their new business. Benn's company – marketing specialists – offered some help in promoting the business and the couple had brochures printed. A friend designed their website for them and, most excitingly, the couple commissioned a luxurious heated swimming pool to be built at the back of the house in their absence.

Life in London remained hectic for Benn and Amy. Both were still working full-time and they were now more keen than ever to spend time with the friends they would shortly be leaving behind to begin their new life in France. The year culminated in their marriage.

'It was a crazy six months,' concludes Amy. 'There just didn't seem to be any time. We were frantically trying to organise the wedding, sort out a business plan *and* get the marketing under way.'

Although the French house, Houtsak Ina, was structurally sound there was work to be done before French Fusion Holidays could open for business. More bathrooms needed to be added to cater for the guest rooms and the whole place desperately needed redecorating. The property had been built in the 1970s and, the couple reckoned, had not been redecorated since.

'It was a big floral headache,' says Amy, wrinkling her nose. 'Although we didn't really plan to get things under way until we moved out there, we did have a brave stab at some decorating prior to this. In June 2002 we headed out to Houtsak Ina with ten mates for a painting party. The idea was that in return for full board, every set of friends would paint the room that they were staying in. It sounds simple enough, but we all failed miserably. Inevitably, the whole adventure just turned into a drinking holiday and we only managed to paint one room between all ten of us. It was enormous fun, though!'

Benn and Amy, now Mr and Mrs Coley, finally moved lock, stock and barrel to Pouillon in February 2003, a year after they had first signed for the house. They arrived with six friends in tow to help unpack and arrange furniture. The pool, despite running dramatically over budget, looked beautiful, but the house was another matter altogether. The Coleys thought that they could cope with decorating the place but, being complete DIY novices, they realised that when it came to installing bathrooms they would need to call in expert help, so they began looking into employing some local builders. Of course there was plenty of work to do, but it wasn't too daunting, so during their first couple of weeks Benn and Amy made plenty of time to properly acquaint themselves with the local area and its attractions. Pouillon is based inland of Biarritz, and so is around half an hour from the beautiful coastline. Something that Benn and Amy hadn't really considered when they bought but that was to prove a boon to their business plans was that they were also just an hour from the mountains. In fact Houtsak Ina boasted beautiful views to the Pyrenees on a clear day. It all seemed perfect.

On day fourteen of their new life, however, things went horribly wrong. Amy and Benn had been enjoying their surroundings by spending a day skiing in the mountains, when Amy took a nasty fall and badly broke her leg.

'I am a really, really careful person,' she comments. 'I rarely do anything active, to be honest; the occasional trip to the gym is all I manage. The shock of having an accident like this was horrific, I just couldn't believe it. I had the plates taken out in February 2004 and I think it is only since then that I have really come to terms with it and considered the chapter closed.'

As well as being a severe blow to Amy personally, the accident also set the business plans back.

'It wasn't too disastrous,' Benn reasons. 'We would have liked to be up and running sooner but we hadn't taken any bookings for holidays at that point so there wasn't any pressure to get the house finished by a certain date. We just held off on the marketing a little to make sure that we wouldn't get any bookings until we were ready. I think we realistically knew at that point that we wouldn't be ready until July.'

'In a way it might have been a good thing,' says Amy optimistically. 'I didn't want Benn doing anything without me because this was our joint project, so really we had this rest period forced upon us. I think we might have run around like headless chickens trying to get stuff ready as soon as possible if things hadn't worked out like this. We just had to be laid-back.'

Amy was bedridden for three weeks and had a cast on for a further six. Although she was in a lot of pain and frustrated by her immobility, she admits her convalescence could have been worse.

'The sun was shining and I had a beautiful pool to sit next to. Once I felt okay again in myself I could hobble outside and concentrate on getting a good tan.'

The break also gave them a chance to practise their French, pretty much unrehearsed since their school days, and to meet some of the local people, with whom they got along famously.

Once Amy had recovered sufficiently, they were able to make progress on the house. By now they had their first booking for the first week in July – they had a deadline. The builders moved in to install the extra bathrooms and put up partition walls, while Amy and Benn cracked on with revamping the outdated interior.

'It didn't take long to realise that we had underestimated how much the refurbishment was going to cost,' says Benn. 'We had £10,000 of savings to cover the work but the bathrooms alone were going to cost £15,000. The total was likely to run to more than £20,000. Fortunately there was a back-up plan.'

Although it was not something that he wanted to do, Benn was able to find freelance work back in England. The skills of a chartered accountant are transferable, and, more importantly, they are applicable remotely. Thus the financial tension was eased by Benn's new income and, more excitingly, by the deposits that were accompanying French Fusion's bookings.

With this potential crisis averted, it wasn't long before the Coleys faced a new one. The pair had thought that not taking any bookings until July would give them plenty of time to get the guest accommodation up to scratch, but things weren't quite panning out.

'Building and decorating work is always painfully slow,' explains Amy. 'I was hopelessly unrealistic. When we first arrived I thought, 'okay eight rooms need decorating, it can't take more than a day to decorate a room, so eight days and I'll be done.' Oh, I was so naive; it took closer to eight months! The builders were great and we have no complaints about the work at all – it all went very smoothly – but we had hoped it would be quicker. Our anxiety really peaked on the morning of the arrival of our first guests. They were on the plane and the guest toilets hadn't yet been plumbed in. I was in tears, walking around just shouting and swearing at everyone, it was awful.'

Amazingly, Benn, Amy and their builders pulled off what had seemed impossible that morning: the guests arrived, Houtsak Ina was immaculate, the toilets were fully functional and a delicious home-cooked dinner was ready for serving.

'Our first clients were here for a corporate weekend, meetings combined with some relaxation and socialising,' recalls Benn. 'It was really nerve-racking. They were actually old colleagues of mine but they had paid the full price so we felt we couldn't relax even though we knew them.'

'That first weekend we had fourteen guests,' continues

Amy. 'It was crazy. I had never catered for fourteen people before and it was seriously hard work.'

In spite of their inexperience and nerves, Benn and Amy remained the perfect hosts all weekend, gaining a whole lot of compliments on the house and the service. But even with their first satisfied customers under their belts, the Coleys didn't feel relaxed.

'Our next guests were complete strangers so we were even more tense. A bus load of strangers were going to turn up on our doorstep expecting to be entertained. Fortunately there were only eight of them so it wasn't nearly so much stress. In fact they were lovely and we ended up having a brilliant time with them.'

A year on and there is no denying that French Fusion holidays has had a strong start. The first summer season brought six weeks of bookings and the low season, though obviously more quiet, brought enough clients to keep the Coleys busy and pay their bills.

'There have been a few surprises,' Benn confesses. 'There is no denying that we underestimated how much work is involved in this business. It can be complete mayhem being at everyone's beck and call twenty-four hours a day. Privacy can be an issue too; we rarely get uninterrupted time together when guests are here.

'Another surprise has been our clients themselves. Don't get me wrong, we have been very lucky and they have all been lovely, but we had expected our market would be DINKYs (dual-income-no-kids-yet couples), but instead we have had far more families than we envisaged. On reflection I think they might be a better market for us: the kids love all the activities – and the parents usually do too.'

There is no doubt that the couple are enjoying the change of pace in Pouillon.

'In a way living here is more sociable than London,' Benn muses. 'It is different, of course. In Wimbledon we knew our closest next-door neighbours and that was it; here we know the whole street and they know us. We have made a big effort from the outset to be sociable, to speak French and to try and fit in – we go to local bars; we use local artisans and suppliers. People have been brilliant and we haven't encountered any negativity at all.'

'We still keep in regular touch with our friends from London too,' adds Amy. 'They come out to see us quite a lot; we have pool parties and fun weekends. Benn goes back to London about once a month because of the freelance work he is still doing, but I don't get back so much. In a way I feel I need to be careful that I don't get too sucked into this lovely relaxing life and become a recluse. I might go a bit stir-crazy sometimes and have to get out, but I find London very claustrophobic these days. The last time I went to a club I almost freaked out . . . I must be growing up!'

Clearly settled and happy in Pouillon, Benn and Amy are beginning to put down further roots there. They plan to buy another house in the town to rent out, which they think will be an excellent investment. Although the area is presently relatively untouched by Brits, it is beautiful and a tourist invasion is inevitable – the Parisians are already starting to snap up second homes in the region, doubling house prices in just over a year. The Coleys also plan to start a family once their busy summer season is over.

'We've got around fifteen weeks of bookings in the summer, which worries me massively,' grins Amy ruefully.

'Two weeks is hard work, I really think this might kill us – not that I'm complaining, you understand. It just didn't really seem like a good time for me to be getting pregnant, so we are going to wait until the rush has died down. We are both very excited, though.'

'To be honest, I think the coming year will be a real test for us,' says Benn. 'Last year the excitement of moving over here was overwhelming and we were happy just wandering around our big house! I think that having the camera crew helped carry us a bit too: they maybe helped us to make deadlines that we might not have otherwise met. This year it is just Amy and me running our business. It will be hard work, but if the past is anything to go by, it will be enormously rewarding. We love life here and have no regrets at all about making the move.'

You can find out more about Benn and Amy Coley, their house Houtsak Ina and their catered activity holidays by visiting their website http://www.frenchfusion.com. Alternatively you can give them a call on +33 558 982 596.

Top Tips

Benn and Amy offer some advice:
- One thing we would definitely recommend is to organise your marketing strategy and website *before* you go. Once you arrive, time and money is just swallowed up with other things, and you will be so grateful that you got it sorted first because marketing is the most important part of any business. It didn't

necessarily pan out for us because we built our whole website before we left and still didn't get any bookings, but at least we didn't have to find time and money to do it among everything else. If you need to make changes, you can always tweak the site or text once it is up and running.

- Learn from the mistakes other people make. The *No Going Back* series is so helpful for that. For example, when we first arrived, we had eight rooms to decorate and thought that it would take eight days – it took eight months. Be reasonable and realistic and think about how long it is going to take and how much it will cost. Again, we had a £10,000 budget for the refurbishment, which actually cost £20,000 – make sure you work it out properly.

- Unless you are positioned right on the beach we think it is pretty imperative to have a pool if you are expecting paying guests. We paid out a lot of money to have a lovely, heated swimming pool installed but it really does pay for itself. The heating means we can open it early and keep it open for longer. It is a big selling point.

- It's that old property mantra again: location, location, location. To do something like us you have to be in a geographical position that has a lot to offer. We were so lucky because we didn't even really consider that when we bought. Pouillon is just an hour from mountains and half an hour from the sea – there aren't many places in the world that can boast that. For proximity to the UK as well, it is a unique location. It is so diverse here that, as far as activities go, we have never had a request that we couldn't cater for. We really can't imagine what you cannot do here!

- Consider the seasonality of what you want to do. We have friends out here that can only have guests in the summer because they don't offer anything other than accommodation and sunshine. The other ten months of the year might sound idyllic but you really can get very bored. The winter is cold and wet just like in Britain – we can't sit around our pools in thirty-degree heat all year round. We are glad that we are able to cater for guests in winter too – it keeps us busy.

- The reference book we used is called *Living and Working in France* by David Hampshire. It is excellent and we recommend it to anyone thinking of moving here.

Budget Sheet

How Benn and Amy funded their move:

Benn and Amy were spurred into buying an overseas property by the receipt of a sizeable inheritance. Even so, the property that they purchased was substantially out of their original price range and required extensive, and costly, renovation work. The gamble paid off, however, and French Fusion holidays is now a thriving business providing a comfortable standard of living for the Coleys and the further work required on Houtsak Ina. Prior to the arrival of the first guests, Benn and Amy had collected around

Credit	Value (£s)
Inheritance	65,000
Savings	10,000
Mortgage on French property	100,000
Loans or other assets	20,000
Rental income per month from Wimbledon flat	1,000
Total	*196,000*

£6500 (€9700) worth of deposits, which paid for the final touches to the property when the savings were running low.

Practical Directory – Landes and Biarritz

Region

Benn and Amy's property is in the Landes region – the second biggest in the whole of France. With a wonderful climate and fantastic scenery, the couple couldn't have chosen a better place from which to run activity holidays. Landes boasts the largest forest in Europe as well as vast nature reserves which are ideal for walking, cycling or horseriding. There are dozens of lakes for fishing and watersports and the nearby Pyrenees mountains provide ample opportunity for skiing and snowboarding in the winter. Houtsak Ina is

Debit	Value (£s)	Value (Euros)
Cost of French property	160,000	238,775
Associated purchase costs	5,000	7,460
Removal costs	2,500	3,730
Renovation costs	20,000	29,847
Cost of heated pool with decking	28,000	41,786
Initial outlay for setting up business	5,000	7,460
Total	220,500	329,058

also just forty minutes outside of Biarritz, a glamorous, cosmopolitan city, renowned the world over for the quality of its waves. The beaches aren't bad either; all in all, 106 kilometres of white sand skirt the coastline. Should you prefer alternative methods of water-related relaxation you could always head inland to one of the thermal springs or spas dotted around the area. For more tourist information visit http://www.tourismelandes.com, http://www.landes.org or http://www.alternative-aquitaine.com.

Culture

As with virtually anywhere in France, gastronomy is a hugely important aspect of life in Landes. The locals are particularly proud of their *foie gras*, made from the liver of free-range ducks and geese, which features in many traditional recipes. Other highlights of the Landes cuisine include asparagus and kiwis, both of which grow exceptionally well in the area.

Amy, however, has been less than impressed with the local cuisine she has encountered.

'It is hardly cordon bleu!' she exclaims. 'On every menu I have seen there is "foot" or "head" or "tongue", which really doesn't appeal to me. It is just good, honest food, I guess. It is not traditionally a wealthy area so they don't like to waste anything.'

Being so close to the Basque countryside and the Spanish border makes this area of the world very interesting culturally. A *mélange* of all these mighty traditions flavour the arts, architecture, music and dance of Landes. The Coleys' house, Houtsak Ina, is built in traditional Landes style. The year is punctuated by festivals which are organised by individual towns and villages and where wonderful displays of flamenco and classical music can be observed – and the locals certainly know how to let their hair down: some of these events last for five days! Bullfighting and Landes-style cow-baiting are very popular in the area too, with events attracting huge interest and excitement. Pouillon has its own bullring where regular spectacles take place.

Transport

Undoubtedly the easiest way to get to Pouillon is to fly to Biarritz or Pau, both of which are only a forty-minute drive. Try Ryanair (http://www.ryanair.com) for cheap flights from London. Air France also fly from the East Midlands, London, Birmingham, Manchester, Bristol, Glasgow, Aberdeen and Edinburgh, among other places: see http://www.airfrance.com for details. There are also international airports in Toulouse, Bordeaux and Bilbao, which are around two hours away. For these routes try British

Airways (http://www.british-airways. com) and easyJet (http://www.easyjet.com).

If you fancy taking the train, the Eurostar departs from Waterloo and takes around nine hours to reach nearby Dax. You can change trains in either Paris or Lille. You can also take the ferry. Bilbao and Santander are just a couple of hours away by car and, although the crossing might be long, there are usually plenty of activities to entertain the kids, which might make your journey far more bearable. See http://www.poferries.com.

Once you have arrived in Landes, excellent train (TGV) services and road networks exist so there will rarely be a problem getting anywhere.

Jobs

Aquitaine (the Region in which the Landes is positioned) has a very high unemployment rate of 10.2 per cent. Agriculture plays a strong role in the economy, whereas the industrial sector is comparatively small despite a dynamic aeronautics and timber industry. Salaries are also slightly lower than those found throughout most of the rest of France. Labour shortages are in the same areas as those experienced across most of Europe. There is a need for IT workers, cooks, waiters and bartenders, construction workers, and – more unusually – for bakers and confectionary makers.

Recruitment

See Chapter 2

House Prices

Even within the eighteen months that Benn and Amy have

lived in Pouillon property prices have increased. The capital gain they have made on their £160,000 outlay is staggering, and in order to buy a similar property now you would need a budget of around £400,000. Typical homes in Landes are called *maison landes* and definitely qualify as character properties. They feature long sloping roofs and balconies. Also available are the *maisons de maître*, which are box-shaped but also highly desirable. Amy and Benn's land is probably of average size for the region; between one and two acres is standard.

More and more British people are moving out to this area of the world, having discovered – as the Coleys did – just how much the area has to offer. Biarritz has always been a honeypot for jet-setters and property prices remain high in line with this popularity and kudos. A high-quality two-bedroom apartment in a key location would carry a price tag of around £350,000 (€522,300), while a substantially smaller two-bedroom apartment away from the seafront could probably be yours for closer to £200,000 (€298,460).

Tax
See Chapter 2

Residency
See Chapter 2

Education
See Chapter 2

Health
See Chapter 2

Useful Contacts

Information in this chapter relating to jobs has come from EURES – the European Job Mobility Portal. For more information on any aspect of living and working abroad visit their website at http://www.europa.eu.int/eures/home. There is also a freephone helpline number: 00800 4080 4080.

Information was also supplied by property agents Latitudes, from whom Benn and Amy bought their property. They can be contacted at the following address:

Latitudes French Property Agents
Grosvenor House
1 High Street
Edgware
Middlesex
HA8 7TA
Tel: 020 8951 5155
Fax: 020 8951 5156
Email: sales@latitudes.co.uk
Website: http://www.latitudes.co.uk

APPENDIX

Getting Started – Some Useful Contacts

There is little doubt that deciding to begin a new life abroad is the beginning of a huge adventure. Pursuing that dream of living out a life in the sun (or snow) and of spending far more quality time with loved ones is a worthy cause indeed, but you have to approach it with realism. As with any undertaking in life, and as we have witnessed in the stories of *No Going Back*, it is not all going to be a bed of roses. There will be hard times wherever you live and whatever you choose to do; Monday mornings happen the world over whether you like it or not!

Of course excitement and anticipation are all part of the experience, but on a more practical level it is wise to do substantial research into both the country and the profession or industry you have chosen. As we have heard from the families featured in this book, you can never fully prepare for all the problems, setbacks and differences that you may experience, but a little homework can stand you in good stead and help you navigate the minefield a little better.

Making the choice

A good starting point is to consult the various magazines and books available on buying property and living abroad. These will often contain stories and case studies from which information can be gleaned, as well as more practical guides to property and destinations. They are also likely to be packed full of useful contacts who can help in your quest. There are plenty of country-specific publications (have a look at the Amazon website or the shelves of WH Smith to find them), but if you fancy reading about a variety of destinations and properties you might want to try something more general like *Homes Overseas* magazine (visit http://www.homesoverseas.co.uk for details). This particular publication comes out monthly and as well as colourful features it offers legal and financial advice.

Next, you might also want to think about visiting an overseas property exhibition. These are held in venues throughout the UK, so there is bound to be one close to you in the near future. These exhibitions usually bring together a wide variety of agents and developers selling property from all over Europe and the rest of the world. There is an informal atmosphere and you can peruse at your leisure, talk to exhibitors face to face and ask all the questions that you prepared earlier. A great advantage for you as a potential buyer is that many agents and developers will have lived in the countries they represent, so you can find out a bit about the culture too. Do make sure that you know what any particular event can offer you before making the effort to attend. Check out the credentials of the organisers and make sure that there will be a good variety of countries and developers on offer; sometimes 'exhibitions' will be more like private shows organised by a single developer or real estate agency. You need to be able to make comparisons in order to find yourself the best deal.

Homes Overseas run exhibitions all over Europe and include a free seminar programme featuring experts speaking on subjects such as finance, investment and the law. To find one near you visit http://www.homesoverseas.co.uk.

Buying a property

Once you have decided on the country and region in which you want to buy, you will need to find a good agent to help you with your search for a property. You may want to check that the agents you use are members of the Federation of Overseas Property Developers, Agents and Consultants (FOPDAC). FOPDAC is a federation of over ninety independent companies specialising in assisting those wishing to purchase abroad. Members include agents, lawyers and financial experts, all of whom meet strict criteria and adhere to a code of ethical practice. For more information on FOPDAC and its members visit http://www.fopdac.com

Before you sign for a property, it is advisable to seek out the services of an international lawyer or solicitor to help you avoid any pitfalls. Buying a house abroad is completely different from buying something in the UK and a lack of familiarity with the system can result in costly mistakes. A lawyer can guide you through the buying process, advising you on crucial issues such as the best form of ownership of the property, contracts, inheritance laws, surveys and tax implications. John Howell & Co. is a specialist firm with over seventeen years' experience of sorting the legal issues involved in foreign home ownership. John Howell heads up the organisation and has also authored the *Sunday Times* guides to buying a property in France, Italy and Spain. He can be contacted at:

John Howell & Co.
Solicitors and International Lawyers
17 Maiden Lane
Covent Garden
London
WC2E 7NL
Tel: +44 (0)20 7420 0400
Fax: +44 (0)20 7836 3626
Website: http://www.europelaw.com
Email: info@europelaw.com

You can find listings of other legal experts on the FOPDAC website.

Settling in and starting up a business

There are numerous helpful contacts listed in the practical directories of this book that will help you obtain the correct paperwork and documents for living and working abroad. Embassies, consulates (both here and in the destination country), Chambers of Commerce, the Inland Revenue and the UK government website are all important sources of information.

For work-related queries, it is probably best to consult with EURES or Jobcentre Plus. The EURES network is specifically designed to facilitate the movement of labour within the European Economic Community, offering advice on CVs, guides to living and working and job listings. Jobcentre Plus is part of the EURES network and each branch will have a EURES advisor to help you out with any queries that you might have about finding work in Europe. Its website also contains useful living and working guides for every EEA member country and useful tips.

Contact details are as follows:

> EURES (The European Job Mobility Portal)
> Helpdesk queries tel: 00800 4080 4080
> Website: http://www.europa.eu.int/eures
>
> Jobcentre Plus
> Jobseeker Direct tel: +44 (0) 845 6060 0234
> Website: http://www.jobcentreplus.gov.uk

NO GOING BACK:
JOURNEY TO MOTHER'S GARDEN

Martin Kirby

No Going Back: Journey to Mother's Garden is the inspirational true story of Martin Kirby and his family, who left the English weather and rat race behind for a new life on an organic farm in Northern Spain.

The Kirby family fell in love with Mother's Garden the moment they saw it: the mottled walls of Mediterranean orange and yellow; the panoramic vistas of the Catalonian countryside; the patchwork land of vines, olive and fig trees. This is their account of the struggles that lay ahead, from the race against time to buy the property to the steep learning curves of speaking Catalan and running a farm. It is a funny, heartfelt memoir about an ordinary family starting over, about gambling everything and making it work.

THE OLIVE FARM

Carol Drinkwater

The Olive Farm is a double love story. It is a lyrical tale of the real-life romance between actress Carol Drinkwater and Michel, a television producer, and of an abandoned Provençal olive farm – Appassionata – which they fall in love with and buy.

And as the olives turn from green to violet, luscious grape-purple to a deep succulent black, we are drawn seductively into Carol and Michel's vibrant Mediterranean world. We experience the highs and lows of Provençal life: the carnivals, customs and local cuisine; the threats of fire, the adoption of a menagerie of animals and a ready-made family; potential financial ruin as well as the thrill of harvesting your own olives by hand – especially when they are discovered to produce the finest extra-virgin olive oil.

Rich and resonant, *The Olive Farm* effortlessly captures the joys of living in a warmer clime, of eating fresh Mediterranean food, swimming in one's own pool, and sharing all this with the love of one's life.

THE OLIVE SEASON
Amour, a new life, and olives too

Carol Drinkwater

Carol Drinkwater's bestselling *The Olive Farm* told the lyrical tale of her real-life romance with partner Michel and an abandoned Provençal olive farm which they fell in love with and bought – a double love story, recounted with wit, warmth and alluring detail.

In *The Olive Season* Carol is now pregnant and their ever-loyal Arab gardener is leaving to oversee the marrying off of his last son. Often unassisted, and with new challenges to face, she takes on the bulk of the farm work alone. Water is , as ever, a costly problem and she goes in search of a diviner who promises almost magical results. But, as the harvest season approaches, dramatic events cast dark shadows over their olive farm.

With magnificent humanity and colourful characters, *The Olive Season* entices readers into Carol and Michel's vibrant Mediterranean world. It is mesmeric and uplifting storytelling.

THE MOON'S OUR NEAREST NEIGHBOUR

Ghillie Başan

Chasing dreams of their own photographic business, Ghillie Başan and her husband Jonathan swap the comfort of their Edinburgh home for Corrunich – a remote cottage at the foot of the Cairngorms.

With jumping cows for company, the Başans begin their new life with no electricity and heavy snowstorms. Generators break down and roads quickly become blocked, but the couple have a series of adventures with a fascinating mix of local farmers, terrified tourists, an African president, and their two babies, Yasmin and Zeki.

The Moon's our Nearest Neighbour is a heartwarming, amusing account of a life lived in the picturesque beauty of highland Scotland; of the ferocious weather and the spectacularly starry skies; and, most of all, of the tremendous strength of spirit in coming to terms with the hardships and isolation of a new lifestyle.

A RIDE IN THE NEON SUN

Josie Dew

'The perfect read for potential backpackers ...
detailed, insightful and often downright hilarious'
Sunday Tribune

It's not easy landing unprepared in a country like
Japan. The eccentricities of the calendar, the alien
alphabet, language and culture have all to be con-
fronted before the disorientated traveller can feel
at ease. Trying to ride a bike through the streets
of one of the most congested cities in the world
would seem to compound your problems.

For Josie Dew, few things could be more challenging – or, for the reader of *A Ride in the Neon Sun*,
more wonderfully entertaining. From Kawasaki to
Kagoshima, Josie discovered a nation rich in dazzling
contrasts. The neon and concrete were there as she
had imagined, but so too were bottomless baths,
love burgers, musical toilet rolls, and a sense of fun
belying the population's rigorous work ethic. Far
from being the reserved race that Josie had heard
about, the Japanese welcomed her with bountiful
smiles and bows – and skin-scorching baths.

'Her painstaking efforts pay off, enabling you
to freewheel effortlessly through this
riveting country' *Time Out*

Other bestselling Time Warner Paperback titles available by mail:

The prices shown above are correct at time of going to press. However, the publishers reserve the right to increase prices on covers from those previously advertised, without further notice.

---

timewarner
paperbacks

TIME WARNER PAPERBACKS
PO Box 121, Kettering, Northants NN14 4ZQ
Tel: 01832 737525, Fax: 01832 733076
Email: aspenhouse@FSBDial.co.uk

POST AND PACKING:
Payments can be made as follows: cheque, postal order (payable to Time Warner Paperbacks) or by credit cards. Do not send cash or currency.

| All UK Orders | **FREE OF CHARGE** |
| EC & Overseas | 25% of order value |

Name (BLOCK LETTERS) . . . .

Address . . . .

. . . .

Post/zip code: . . . .

☐ Please keep me in touch with future Time Warner publications

☐ I enclose my remittance £ . . . .

☐ I wish to pay by Visa/Access/Mastercard/Eurocard

Card Expiry Date
